A personal account of one woman's experience

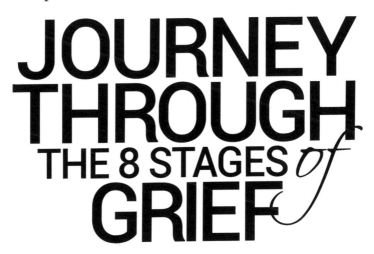

Tammy Packard Hoffman

Copyright © 2015 by Tammy Packard Hoffman. All rights reserved.

Published by Journey Lake Books

Cover and interior design by www.DesignsDoneNow.com
Edited by Kyla Crowther
Cover photo by Tammy Hoffman
Portrait photo by Laurel Hoffman

Scripture quotations are from: The New International Version Study Bible (1985) by Zondervan Bible Publishers and www.blueletterbible.org NIV version.

No part of this book may be reproduced in any form or by any electronic or mechanical means including information storage and retrieval systems—except in the case of brief quotations embodied in critical articles or reviews—without permission in writing from its publisher, Journey Lake Books, 3662 Asperwood Circle, Coconut Creek, FL 33073.

This publication is designed to provide accurate and authoritative information in regard to the subject matter covered. It is sold with the understanding that neither the publisher nor the author is engaged in rendering legal, accounting, or other professional service. If legal advice, psychological advice, or other expert assistance is required, the services of a competent professional person should be sought.—Adapted from a Declaration of Principles Jointly Adopted by a Committee of the American Bar Association and a Committee of Publishers and Associations.

All brand names and product names used in this book are trademarks, registered trademarks, or trade names of their respective holders. Journey Lake Books is not associated with any product or vendor in this book.

Library of Congress Cataloging-in Publication Data

Hoffman, Tammy Packard
Journey Through the 8 Stages of Grief
1. Self-Help 2. Personal Growth 3. Religious 4. Heath, mind and body
ISBN 13: 978-1505808506
Printed in the United States of America.

To my wonderful daughters,
Laurel & Lindsay,
who have triumphed through this tragedy
by God's grace and faithfulness,
and have grown to be incredible, motivated, disciplined,
humorous, and beautiful young women.

ACKNOWLEDGMENTS

I would like to acknowledge all of the wonderful people who stood by me during my grieving and taught me how to serve others in their time of need. Without their love and support I would not have made it through this ordeal.

My family—
My sisters, *Christy Evans* and *Cyndi Dunn*, and their families
Gary's siblings, *Julie Underhill* and *Greg Hoffman*, and their families
My mother, *Patricia Hartmann*, and my late stepfather, *Richard Hartmann*
My father, *Ray Packard*, and stepmother, *Barbara Komorowski*
My in-laws, *Sandy* and *Dave Hoffman*

My stepbrothers—
Jim Hartmann, John Hartmann, and *Tom Hartmann*, and their families

My relatives—
The *Richard Hoffman, Ed Hoffman,* and *Al Lamberti* families

My extended family members—
the *Hoffman, Packard, Elliott* and *McDonald* families
My pastors and youth leaders—
Dr. Ross Bair, the late *Dr. Joseph Scharer*, *Rev. Mark Bolhofner*, *Dr. Dale Goodman*, and *Mrs. Jennie Tchilinguirian*

My counselor, *Diane Pearce*

My church family at The First Presbyterian Church of Coral Springs, especially the following people—
The *Wills Ryan Family*
The late *Conrad Beton Family*
The *Brad Lindbergh Family*
The late *Jeff O'Keefe Family*
The *Bob Graumann Family*
The *Bob Evans Family*
The *Jim Bowman Family*
Mrs. *Karen Bieniek-Tobin*

Also a special thanks to those who encouraged me and helped me get this book published: *Sharon Holt, Brett Hagler, Kyla Crowther, Mick Weltin,* and *Lisa Knight*

TABLE OF CONTENTS

	INTRODUCTION..1
CHAPTER 1	GRIEF BEGINS WITH AN ACCIDENT
	Explanation...9
	Practical Advice...16
	Bible Verses...22
CHAPTER 2	ASSURANCE AND INSURANCE
	Explanation...25
	Practical Advice...30
	Bible Verses...32
CHAPTER 3	STAGE ONE: SHOCK
	Explanation...35
	Journal Entries..39
	Practical Advice...40
	Bible Verses...44
CHAPTER 4	STAGE TWO: EMOTION
	Explanation...47
	Journal Entries..50
	Practical Advice...60
	Bible Verses...70
CHAPTER 5	STAGE THREE: DEPRESSION AND LONELINESS
	Explanation...73
	Journal Entries..78
	Practical Advice...86
	Bible Verses...92

CHAPTER 6	STAGE FOUR: PHYSICAL SYMPTOMS OF DISTRESS	
	Explanation	95
	Journal Entries	98
	Practical Advice	100
	Bible Verses	103
CHAPTER 7	STAGE FIVE: CONSUMED WITH LOSS	
	Explanation	105
	Journal Entries	107
	Practical Advice	114
	Bible Verses	118
CHAPTER 8	STAGE SIX: GUILT	
	Explanation	121
	Journal Entries	124
	Practical Advice	126
	Bible Verses	128
CHAPTER 9	STAGE SEVEN: ANGER AND RESENTMENT	
	Explanation	131
	Journal Entries	141
	Practical Advice	150
	Bible Verses	154
CHAPTER 10	STAGE EIGHT: GRADUAL ACCEPTANCE	
	Explanation	157
	Journal Entries	160
	Practical Advice	164
	Bible Verses	168
	FINAL WORDS	171
	REFERENCES	173

*Sometimes He calms the storm
With a whispered, "Peace be still"
He can settle any sea
But it doesn't mean He will
Sometimes He holds us close
And lets the wind and waves go wild
Sometimes He calms the storm
And other times He calms His child.*
(Wood, 1995)

INTRODUCTION

If you are reading this book, probably you or someone close to you is dealing with a loss right now. I want you to know that I am truly sorry that you are encountering this. I know it is difficult and I can empathize with the pain you are experiencing while you are grieving. I understand this is a challenging time but it is important for you to realize that there is hope for you. There are some things you should know about this process, which is why I have written this book. By educating yourself on the emotions you will encounter, and taking steps to help yourself and others, you will be able to successfully navigate through this difficult time in your life.

Unfortunately, loss is inevitable during our lives. Some situations will occur which will take us by surprise, even if we dreaded that they would happen one day. Other situations will be expected, but will still be difficult for us to handle when they happen.

Loss comes in many shapes and sizes, such as:
- Death of a loved one
- Relationship ending
- Military deployment for yourself or a loved one
- Personal injury or illness
- A loved one's health issues
- A loved one's substance abuse
- Divorce
- Separation
- Miscarriage
- Abortion
- Move

- Change of career/job
- Loss of high-powered career or position
- Conflicts at church or other organization
- Change in financial status (incurring debt, foreclosure, bankruptcy, etc.)
- Children moving out of the house
- Children moving back into the house
- Elderly parents aging
- Elderly parents or relative(s) moving into the house
- Retirement (either you or your spouse)
- Natural disaster

Situations which are not as severe as the previous list, but also result in a sense of loss may include:

- Trip to the Emergency Room
- Accident causing injury
- Car breaking down
- Receiving bad news
- Financial loss
- Losing a sporting event
- Rejection

Obviously this is not a comprehensive list; there are many other factors which can trigger grieving. It is highly likely we will experience several difficult situations during our lifetime which will cause us to grieve. Although the circumstances can span a wide range of situations, any loss will result in experiencing a series of emotions known as "The Grieving Process." These are eight emotional and physical stages we encounter after a traumatic experience. Whenever we lose something of value to us or experience a change in our circumstances which causes stress, we are likely to experience portions or all of "The Grieving Process."

When my husband died without any warning, my life changed dramatically. One minute my husband was sitting next to me, and the next minute he was taken from me, never to return. In the days, weeks, and months following his death, I had a preconceived idea of how I should grieve. However, my expectations of how I thought I should grieve and how I actually felt differed radically. This dichotomy resulted in confusion and guilt, until I learned that when we go through difficult times, we experience "The Grieving Process." What a relief it was for me to realize that the feelings I was experiencing were normal.

Because understanding the process was incredibly helpful to me, I want to pass along this knowledge, as well as my personal experience, to you. It is my hope that from the material in this book you will know what to expect during the difficult times in your life. Hopefully, you will be encouraged to know that the emotions discussed in this book are normal, and that if you choose to work through them, you will be able to move successfully through each stage. Scott (1992) states, "It's also important to remember that grieving is a process, and that it will end one day, as unlikely as this seems now."

Grieving impacts not just individuals, but entire families and communities. While members of the group who are closer to the trauma will suffer more intensely, other family and friends will also experience some of the emotions described in this book. To illustrate, if the traumatic event, such as a death, was written on paper and a circle was put around it, then concentric circles could be placed around this circle. The people who are closest to the person would be in the first concentric circle, because they are feeling the most pain. People who are not as close to the person would be put in circles which are farther away from the center. Their location would depend on how close they were to the person who died. They are suffering, but not as intensely as the people who were closest to the deceased.

This point reminds us that while as individuals we grieve, the families, congregations, and communities which we belong to grieve also. While it is comforting to know we are not alone in our grief, it is important to realize that our family members and friends, who may have different personalities than we do, are likely to grieve differently than we do. Since many complex emotions are involved in grieving we should be patient with one another during this time (Anderson, 2009, p. 127).

This book is designed to help all who are grieving, as well as family and friends who want to help the bereaved. Due to our diverse personalities and the nature of our loss, each person grieves uniquely. We might not go through the stages in order, and we might not experience every stage, although we will experience at least two of the stages. Most likely we will not spend the same amount of time in each stage, and we may find that some of the stages overlap. We may return to one or more stages several times before we work through it. We must work through our grief at our own pace and not be rushed by our own or other's opinions of what the time frame should be. If we do work through our grief we should reach the ultimate stage of "Acceptance" (Kuebler-Ross, 1969).

This book covers eight different stages of "The Grieving Process."

In the interest of helping my readers work through the stages of grief and successfully reach "Acceptance," I have divided each chapter of this book into four useful parts:

EXPLANATION: The first part defines and explains a particular stage of grieving. Although knowledge of what is to come does not lessen the pain, it will prepare you to know what you can expect.

JOURNAL ENTRIES: The next part contains entries from my personal journal which I kept after my husband died. Looking back at these entries I am embarrassed about some of the things I wrote, however I tried not to edit them because they were my actual thoughts and feelings at the time. Perhaps those of you who are grieving are struggling with similar emotions, and will be able to relate to how I felt. The entries are not always in chronological order, since I did not go through the stages in order.

PRACTICAL ADVICE: The third section of each chapter gives practical advice to both those who are grieving and also to friends and family who want to help. When we are grieving, there are steps we can take to help ourselves work through each stage. It is not healthy to stay in any stage longer than necessary. Hopefully, these recommendations will help you successfully and efficiently transition through each stage. In addition, I witnessed countless acts of kindness from my wonderful family, friends, and even complete strangers. My desire it to pass this wisdom onto family members and friends who want to help but feel inept.

BIBLE VERSES: The fourth part of each chapter shares Bible verses which I found comforting and encouraging, and I would like to pass them onto others who are hurting, also.

My purpose in breaking each chapter into these sections is to try to make this book a user-friendly handbook during your grieving process. I encourage you to read the portions of the book which help you.

In our times of sorrow we move either closer to God, or farther away from Him. My prayer for you is that you increase your faith and see God working through this process. Romans 8:28 tells us, "And we know that in all things God works for the good of those who love him, who have been called according to his purpose." God is using your grief to work in you. You may not appreciate the way He is doing it (in fact, you may not understand any of this and actually hate the means). My hope is that you know that our sovereign heavenly Father is still in control, He is still faithful, and He still loves you. I hope that you not only know this, but that you are able to experience God's presence and love during this dark time in your life. Anything that draws us closer to God is a good thing (although it definitely may not seem like it at the time).

God is going to teach you a great deal about Himself and also about yourself during these next few months, lessons you would not have learned if you were not pushed to the limit. God can use these circumstances to help you grow stronger in your faith and become a better person. That may not be very comforting to you right now. It wasn't comforting to me, either, at the time. In fact, to be honest, I didn't like it at all.

During this time, I encourage you to pray this prayer that David wrote in Psalm 86:11, "Teach me your way, O Lord, and I will walk in your truth; give me an undivided heart, that I may fear your name." Please trust that God can work in and through you in a mighty way during this horrendous time of your life.

Again, please know that I am truly sorry for your loss. I have been through a similar situation, and I know that loss is extremely difficult. My prayer is that this book will encourage you and help you know what to expect so you can successfully transition through each stage of "The Grieving Process" as you work through your grief.

> **It was extremely comforting to know I was not alone in my grief.**

CHAPTER 1

GRIEF BEGINS WITH AN ACCIDENT

"Can you tell me where the pain is?" an unfamiliar voice asked me. I could not respond. Lying on my back, I was trying to focus, but everything seemed cloudy in my confused, semi-conscious state. Slowly, I became coherent, and some details from the evening started flowing back into my memory. My mind recalled a conversation I'd had earlier in the evening with my husband, Gary.

"I don't want to go; I'm so tired. Let's just stay home." Gary sounded weary as he sat on the edge of our bed. He had spent the past two days flying private charters from Fort Lauderdale to the island of Bimini in the Bahamas. It was one of the many odd jobs he had been doing since his position as a Boeing 727 flight engineer ended when the airline he worked for had gone bankrupt six months earlier.

"Oh, no, it's too late; we can't cancel. And I really want to go," I responded, throwing him a pleading look from my position in front of the bathroom mirror where I was finishing my hair.

"But I'm so wiped out. Can't we just stay home?" he reiterated. Besides the two flights, he had worked hard during the week on construction sites for his Dad's plumbing company.

I understood his exhaustion. I, too, had been busy. Along with taking care of our two daughters, Laurel, age two, and Lindsay, nine months, I had helped at our church's annual Vacation Bible School program all week. Earlier in the day, I had also cleaned my father-in-law's office, and then our house, like I did every Saturday. I was definitely tired, but I really wanted to attend this Bible Study for young couples.

Lately, we had not had many opportunities to get out socially due to our hectic schedules and tight finances. I loved our two children and this stage of our lives, yet all week I had been looking forward to dressing up in the new outfit Gary had given me for my recent twenty-seventh birthday and going out with him to converse with other adults.

Gary wandered into the living room and rescued tow-headed Lindsay from her playpen, which was placed in front of our sliding glass door. We could see the sun just beginning to set, creating streaks of gold, purple, pink and blue on the horizon. The colors played softly off the reflection of the small lake behind our house. Some hotel rooms are larger than our tiny two-bedroom, two-bath abode, yet it was our first home and we loved it, although we were struggling financially to hang on to it since Gary had lost his job.

"Oh, c'mon," I cajoled, "this is only our third time going to this group. The babysitter is due in fifteen minutes, and we are supposed to bring the sodas. We can't cancel now."

"All right," Gary conceded, "but only if you promise we can leave early."

I agreed. After instructing our sitter, Gary's teenage cousin who lived in our neighborhood, we headed out the door to our ten-year-old, very used car.

"I'll drive," I offered.

Gary shook his head, his fine, straight blond hair falling around his blue eyes as he slid into the driver's seat. We had just celebrated our eighth anniversary, and I thought he just kept getting better looking with age. I, on the other hand, still had ten stubborn pounds to lose after my last pregnancy, which I found hard to camouflage on my five-foot, one-inch frame. In addition, my blond hair had turned brown and my body had rearranged in certain areas, something all those maternity books had failed to mention.

Hearing the nurse brought me back to the present. "Try to relax; the doctor will be in shortly."

"Do you smell beer?" I asked the nurse weakly, confused by the fermented, alcoholic smell in the midst of this sanitary environment.

She nodded. "Do you drink?"

"No," I replied, still not making a connection. "We do not drink. We were on our way to a Bible study."

I had become a Christian at age fourteen. Three years later, I met Gary at our church's youth group and we began to date. We never drank alcohol.

"You have company," the nurse announced. My sister-in-law, Karin, came over to my side, a concerned expression masking her normally effervescent personality.

"Is Gary dead?" I asked her bluntly.

"No," she answered, looking shocked. She gently explained that we had been in a car accident and we had been taken to different hospitals. That was all she knew about our situation.

As she stayed by my side, nurses and doctors moved efficiently in and out of my cubicle, explaining their procedures to my groggy, uncomprehending mind. They determined exploratory surgery was necessary to locate and stop my internal bleeding and they began to prepare me for surgery.

I kept asking the staff for an update on Gary's status, but no one seemed to have any news.

Then our elderly pastor entered. Slowly, he walked over and stood beside my bed, clasping the cold, metallic rail between his hands.

"How is Gary doing?" I questioned him.

He cleared his throat. "Tammy, dear—" he started in a fatherly voice. The emptiest feeling came over me. I already knew.

"Gary passed on, didn't he?" I interrupted.

"I'm afraid so," he responded softly.

"He didn't want to go out tonight; I made him go."

He began speaking some words of comfort to me, but I could not hear them. It was like he was speaking a foreign language.

I was in such shock and confusion that I could not even cry. My thoughts vacillated between disbelief and panic. Later, I learned that less than five miles from our home, a drunk driver had run a red light and broad-sided our car, slamming into my husband's door. The driver's small pick-up truck then flipped over our car. During this collision, his open containers of beer had sprayed on us. When the truck landed, he was crushed beneath it. The drunk driver died at the scene.

Gary also passed away at the scene, but the paramedics were able to revive him. Although I had no memory of the accident, I must have realized then that he would probably not survive. He was airlifted to the nearest hospital with a trauma center. On his way to surgery, his heart stopped.

I did not want to live now, either. What was the point? Then I thought of my girls. I realized it would be devastating for them to lose one parent, let alone two. I had to hang on for their sake.

Final preparations were made, and the surgeon performed the exploratory surgery, removing my ruptured spleen.

After my surgery I was moved into Intensive Care. Family and friends began arriving. I drifted in and out of consciousness for the next couple of days, only dimly aware of the world around me. My mom and step-dad drove three hours from the marina where they had been spending the weekend on their boat. Gary's sister, Julie, came down from the Florida panhandle. Even in my drowsy state, I recalled that she was six months pregnant, and wondered if she was handling the news okay. My dad arrived from New York. My step-brother, John, and older sister, Cyndi, came to help. Aunts, uncles, and cousins arrived from Indiana and New York. Flowers were delivered constantly.

My younger sister, Christy, was like a pit bull; she came immediately and could not be torn from my side. Devastated for me, she stubbornly refused to listen to any reasoning that she should take a break. Finally, the family and staff succumbed to her wishes and a kind nurse arranged to have a roll-away cot brought into my room for her to sleep on at night.

Gary's brother, Greg, and his family were making the funeral arrangements. They would consult me periodically, but nothing seemed to make sense to me, which left it to them to make all of the painful decisions. I did ask them to make the funeral as late as possible so I could attend. They were able to hold it off for a week.

Three days later, I returned to full consciousness, but the doctors would not release me at that point. Along with recovering from surgery, I was dealing with injuries including a concussion, three broken ribs, a bruised lung, and a hairline fracture in my pelvis. They eventually agreed to release me to go to the funeral and I returned home to my daughters on Thursday evening. I had only one day to prepare for Friday night's viewing. The funeral service was scheduled for Saturday.

Due to the physical and emotional trauma, I had lost thirteen pounds in the hospital. Since I did not have any clothes that fit me, Karin kindly went shopping and picked out several dresses for me to choose from to wear to the viewing and the funeral. Additionally, she sorted through our family photos and framed several to put on display in the funeral home.

During the private family viewing hour I wandered around the room on crutches, looking at the pictures and the flowers. The hour was coming to a close, but I still had not gone up to the open casket. Christy, still by my side, came with me. I looked at Gary's lifeless body, which just one week before had been so vibrant. I could not believe it. Makeup on his face, his hair arranged wrong, eyes sewn shut; it was surreal.

Friends soon swarmed in. Someone flipped open a wheelchair and led me to it. My dad came over and stood by my side to support me emotionally. A line of visitors formed, and for three hours, visitors came non-stop, first going to the casket and then coming over to me. It was extremely comforting to know I was not alone in my grief.

The next day, I was exhausted, moving slowly, and as usual, running late. The church was already overflowing when we arrived for the funeral service. After the ceremony, my family joined me in the limo that led the procession to the cemetery. Looking out the window, I saw a long line of cars snaking behind us.

When we arrived at the cemetery, the cars halted to a stop near the grave. A small tent with chairs had been set up. The men from the funeral parlor unloaded the casket and set it down gently, laying an arrangement of flowers on top of it. The sight of the casket lying near the empty grave began to sink in. A feeling of panic rushed over me; I felt like someone had hit my stomach with a baseball bat. I wanted to scream, *Don't put him in there! You can't leave him here! This can't be happening!* But I swallowed the words, choked back the tears and tried to regain my composure, feeling I must be strong for everyone else.

Practical Advice for Funerals

FOR THOSE WHO ARE GRIEVING:

1. Make funeral arrangements.
This is a difficult necessity. Ask for help if you need it. Do not try to handle everything by yourself if you cannot. Realize that many people desire to help you, but do not know how. Feel free to ask them and tell them specifically what you need help with.

2. Time events together. A visitation often precedes the funeral. Be aware that each event will be extremely stressful and draining. After attending several funerals, I recommend putting all of the events together (visitation, funeral, and reception) on the same day, if possible. This allows you to get everything over at once, instead of dragging it out. Obviously, the logistics of the situation need to be considered when making the arrangements.

3. Be considerate of others. Realize that you are not the only one grieving over your loss; other family members and friends are hurting as well. Try to be considerate and accommodating to their needs and desires, too. Because all of the family members are stressed, other issues may surface at this time. If this happens, try to diffuse the situation. You might explain that you realize you need to deal with this issue, but this is not the best time. Ask their permission to speak about it again after the funeral events have passed. It would be helpful for the family to be unified, not fragmented, during this difficult time. Be especially careful of your words and actions right now; they could do long-term damage.

4. Consider taking medications. Weigh the pros and cons of taking medication for the funeral. My doctor prescribed Valium, which I took. In retrospect, I probably still had morphine in my system from my hospital stay. Because of these drugs, I was fairly foggy at the funeral. Painkillers will obviously dull the pain, and probably help you to better maintain your composure. One of the negative effects is that you may feel pretty out of touch with the events.

5. Locate life insurance policies. Be aware that your loved one's life insurance policies may exist not only through life insurance companies, but also through his/her employer, mortgage company, and credit card companies.

> **PRACTICAL ADVICE**

6. Contact Social Security. Social Security Survivors Benefits provides income for the families of workers who die. Ninety-eight out of every 100 children whose working parent has passed away can qualify for benefits. Widows, widowers, dependent children, and parents can receive Social Security Survivors benefits and a small one-time death payment. The Social Security website encourages you to contact your nearest Social Security office or visit www.ssa.gov as soon as possible after the death of a loved one, even if you do not yet have all of the required information.

.

Practical Advice for Funerals

FOR FAMILY AND FRIENDS OF THOSE GRIEVING:

1. Help with funeral arrangements. If help is needed with the funeral planning or logistics, please provide it. Let those who have lost a loved one do as much as they possibly can for themselves (see Chapter 3—Shock for more details). Depending on how close you are to the family, you may offer to go to the funeral home to help make decisions with them, or even go just for moral support.

2. Be a "Personal Shopper." Having my sister-in-law shop for me was an enormous help. I could hardly get out of the hospital, much less to a store to try on clothes. She bought several dresses in a variety of styles and sizes, and even returned those I did not use. You could help the family members get their clothes ready for the event, either by shopping for them or preparing clothes they already own (laundering, dry cleaning and/or ironing). They may also need help with daily errands that they are not able to get to at this time, such as picking up groceries or prescriptions.

3. Provide food. The morning after the accident, food came pouring in to my house (where my parents were staying with my daughters) and my in-laws' house. What a tremendous help this was! We did not feel like eating, much less cooking, but we needed to feed ourselves as well as our out-of-town family and funeral guests. People brought an assortment of food—meat dishes, casseroles, salads, side dishes, pastas, snacks, fruit, and desserts. If you live out of town, you can order food to be delivered, such as a fruit basket.

4. Attend the viewing and funeral. After losing a loved one, I now understand how much it means when people reach out to those who are grieving. The blockbuster attendance at my husband's viewing and funeral was extremely comforting to my whole family. It is not pleasant to attend these functions, but it is a wonderful way to show your love and encouragement to the family.

5. Send flowers. Several people sent flowers to the funeral home and even to me in the hospital and at home. Again, that meant so much to our family.

6. Send cards. Cards also came pouring in, and many contained money, which was extremely generous and helpful. Some of the most meaningful cards came from people I did not know. One was from a former co-worker of Gary's, a lady whom I had never even met. In her card, she wrote a little note telling me she was impressed that he had quit his previous job because it interfered with his family time. I was grateful that she took the time to share this with me. Many other people included a personal note in which they shared something specific they admired about Gary. I found those notes to be so encouraging and thoughtful. It was comforting to see how much my husband meant to others.

7. Look into Social Security Survivors Benefits. Bereaved people probably do not have the clarity of mind or the stamina to attend to this right now, so perhaps you can help them by researching and making an appointment for them at the Social Security Office after the funeral. You might also help by determining what paperwork is needed, and then help them gather it.

8. Be available. Some victims may prefer not to be left alone right now. I had one friend who, during the week after her husband died, informed me that the whole family wanted to do everything together. Someone wanted ice cream from the grocery store, so all ten of them loaded into a van and went to the store together! This will probably pass, but for now, if they want your company, please stay with them.

> After losing a loved one,
> I now understand how much
> it means when people reach out
> to those who are grieving.

Bible Verses

TO COMFORT DURING A LOSS:

*He (the Lord) heals the brokenhearted
and binds up their wounds.*
Psalm 147:3

*"Naked I came from my mother's womb,
and naked I will depart.
The Lord gave and the Lord has taken away;
may the name of the Lord be praised."
In all this, Job did not sin
by charging God with wrongdoing.*
Job 1:21-22

*God has said, "Never will I leave you;
never will I forsake you."*
Hebrews 13:5

*There is a time for everything,
and a season for every activity under heaven:
a time to be born and a time to die,
a time to plant and a time to uproot,
a time to kill and a time to heal,
a time to tear down and a time to build.
a time to weep and a time to laugh,
a time to mourn and a time to dance.*
Ecclesiastes 3:1-4

God is our refuge and strength,
an ever-present help in trouble
Therefore we will not fear, though the earth give way
and the mountains fall into the heart of the sea,
though its waters roar and foam
and the mountains quake with their surging.
Psalm 46:1-3

Job's wife said to him, "Are you still holding on
to your integrity? Curse God and die!"
He replied, "You are talking like a foolish woman.
Shall we accept good from God, and not trouble?"
In all this, Job did not sin in what he said.
Job 2:9-10

Consider it pure joy, my brothers,
whenever you face trials of many kinds,
because you know that the testing of your faith
develops perseverance.
Perseverance must finish its work
so that you may be mature and complete,
not lacking anything.
James 1:2-4

BIBLE VERSES

> Christianity is not based
> merely on faith,
> but it is also based on facts.

CHAPTER 2

ASSURANCE AND INSURANCE

There are two things you should definitely have in your life, which is why I put this chapter at the beginning of the book: assurance, which is knowing who God is and what He does for you, and insurance, which is taking care of the financial needs of those you leave behind.

You do not need to go through times of suffering alone! The Bible tells us in Psalm 46:1, "God is our refuge and strength, an ever-present help in trouble." You can ask God to help you. But not just any god; the God of Christianity. Since there are many religions which have committed, sincere followers, how can we be certain that Christianity is the true religion? Fortunately, Christianity is not based merely on faith, but it is also based on facts. Let's consider some of the many facts which show Christianity is the only true religion. The Christian Bible has endured over 4000 years, Christianity is the only religion which can prove their God was raised from the dead, and Christianity is the only religion which does not require people to work to go to heaven.

Consider the history of the Christian Bible. It contains 66 books which were written over a period of 1500 years by 40 authors. Given the diversity of the authors and the time span in which it was written, it is remarkable that their points are unified. Without contradicting the other authors, each author continues the same theme, which is God's plan to redeem His people from sin (Geisler, 1996, p. 257).

Since this book has endured for all of these years, some people wonder how we can be assured that the Bible we read today is the same as the original Bible which was written many years ago. Fortunately, evidence, known as "The Dead Sea Scrolls," was found between the years of 1947-1956. These scrolls confirmed that the Bible we have today is the very same one which was written over 4000 years ago. These ancient documents were found in clay jars in 11 caves located on the northwest side of the Dead Sea, 13 miles from Jerusalem. When translated, it was found that these scrolls contained portions and even entire chapters of the Old Testament. When these translations were compared with today's Bible, they confirmed that the writing on the scrolls was the exact same message that is found in the Bibles we have today (McDowell, 2011). This evidence proves the authenticity of our Bible.

Not only has the Bible endured and been found to be accurate and consistent in its message, but no other religion can prove that their god has been raised from the dead. Christianity is the only religion which has evidence that their God, Jesus, rose from the dead. There are over 300 prophecies in the Old Testament, such as Psalm 22:1, Psalm 22:14-18, and Isaiah 53, which Jesus fulfilled. Written several hundred years before Jesus was even born, these prophecies predicted when and how the Messiah would come to earth, what he would do while on earth, and how he would die. In addition to the Old Testament prophets, Jesus also prophesized about his own death, resurrection, and ascension during his ministry on earth. All of these prophecies were fulfilled when, as predicted, Jesus suffered and died on the cross. The Bible explains in Romans 5 why Jesus died on the cross; he did it to take the punishment for all of our sins.

Before removing Jesus' body from the cross a Roman soldier pierced his side with a sword and blood and water came out, proving that Jesus' body was clinically dead. After his body was placed in a tomb, Roman guards were stationed at the entrance of the tomb to assure that no one stole his body to fabricate a story about his resurrection.

When Jesus rose from the dead after being in the tomb for three days, he made appearances over a period of 40 days, and during that time over 500 people witnessed his return to earth. It is also important to note that it really was his physical body which rose from the dead, proven by the fact that he ate bread and fish with his disciples, and Thomas, his doubting disciple, saw Jesus and realized he was able to touch Jesus. A ghost, apparition, or hallucination cannot eat nor be touched.

Jesus' disciples were so assured of his resurrection that after they witnessed Jesus ascending into heaven, they boldly and courageously preached about him for the rest of their lives, and all but one of them died a martyr's death for their beliefs.

In addition to this proof, Christianity is the most loving and merciful religion. If you think God can't empathize with your suffering, realize that Jesus endured extreme suffering when he died on the cross and took the punishment for all of our sins, and God endured extreme suffering when He witnessed the cruelty and pain His son suffered on the cross. Why did they do this? As John 3:16 tells us, "For God so loved the world that He gave His one and only son, that whoever believes in him shall not perish but have eternal life." God and Jesus made this incredible sacrifice to demonstrate the magnitude of their love for us.

John 14:6 also tells us, "Jesus answered, 'I am the way and the truth and the life. No one comes to the Father except through me.'" This verse states that not all faiths lead to heaven. Only faith in Jesus will allow us to go to heaven and be with God when we die.

Another amazing fact about God's incredible love for us is that while other religions require their followers to work in order to earn their way into heaven, Christianity is the only religion where God offers forgiveness of sins and heaven to His followers as a free gift. This is amazing grace!

How do we get this gift? We accept this gift from God by trusting in Jesus Christ alone for cleansing us from our sins and offering us eternal life in heaven. We can do this by saying a simple prayer telling God we believe in Him, we confess we have sinned and we realize we cannot get to heaven by our own efforts. Then thank Him for His free gifts of forgiveness of our sins, His help here on Earth, and eternal life in heaven when we die, and accept these gifts now.

Once we do this, we need to cultivate our relationship with God by praying (which is when we speak to God), reading the Bible (which is when God speaks to us), attending church, fellowshipping with other Christians, serving God, and sharing our faith with others.

God demonstrated His amazing love for us, and He does not want us to go through our suffering alone. Accepting this gift invites Him into our life and allows Him to help us through every situation we encounter.

Not only do we need this assurance of God's love, but if we are an adult we need life insurance. Our loved ones do not need the additional burden of financial stress when we die. How would your death affect the finances of the ones you leave behind?

If you do not already have life insurance or you do not have an adequate amount, I strongly encourage you to take care of this TODAY. Term life insurance can be purchased fairly inexpensively.

In order to help your family, determine how much money they would need for future expenses if you were to die. Include money to cover their monthly expenses, pay off a mortgage, if you have one, or buy a home, if you are renting and planning to buy in the future. It is also prudent to include money to take care of any upcoming events, such as college tuitions, weddings, or retirement. A good insurance agent can help you with these plans.

If you receive health benefits through your employer, you probably have a small life insurance policy already, and you might be able to buy additional life insurance at an affordable rate.

It is also helpful to create a will. Having a plan for the property and money you leave for your loved ones would be extremely beneficial to them. It could also save them time, money, and the frustration that would ensue if there were no will in place and your family has to go to court to work out how to divide your estate. If you do not have a will in place when you die, you are considered to have died intestate, and the court will determine who gets what after your debts are paid. If you want to have a say in this you should create a will.

It may be uncomfortable to discuss this information now, but it is essential for a family who has just lost a loved one to have access to a plan that was created when everyone was thinking clearly. A grieving family does not need the excess burden of a financial strain, whether it is due to insufficient income or a sudden influx of life-insurance money without a well-devised plan to avoid wasting it. Taking these financial steps now could alleviate a great deal of stress after the death of a loved one.

It is important to make both decisions NOW. We are not guaranteed tomorrow (as we know more than anyone!). Therefore, I recommend you do not delay on either one.

Practical Advice for Assurance and Insurance

FOR THOSE WHO ARE GRIEVING:

1. Have assurance. Be assured of your relationship with God. If you have not prayed to accept Jesus as your Lord and Savior, what is stopping you? Life can be difficult, as we well know. I encourage you not to try to walk through it alone. God loves us and wants to have a personal relationship with us.

2. Have insurance. You probably want to take care of those left behind in case of your death, or a family member's death. A death in the family is enough trauma; do not leave your loved ones with a financial burden as well.

3. Make a will. If you do not already have one, you really need to make a will to be sure that your assets go to the right people, and will not be delayed due to "red tape." If your will is old, you should consider updating it. This can be done for a reasonable cost. You can create a simple will on the Internet for less than $50.00.

4. Attend to the above immediately! Do not delay. The above items require a little bit of labor, but all three are extremely important.

Practical Advice for Assurance and Insurance

FOR FAMILY AND FRIENDS OF THOSE GRIEVING:

1. Have assurance and insurance. You have seen firsthand what your family member or friend is going through. Determine to make preparations for your own life as soon as possible.

2. Make a will. Do you have a will, and is it up-to-date? This is important for you, too.

3. Follow up in these two areas. Procrastination can be a big problem for those grieving right now. It may be difficult for them to just get through the day, much less do anything extra. Encourage them to take care of these two areas, and offer any assistance you can. For instance, if they do not have an insurance agent, but you do, you could give them the phone number. You could also follow up with them in a week to see if they have taken care of this matter.

Bible Verses

THAT ASSURE US OF SALVATION AND ETERNITY:

*Jesus declared, "I tell you the truth,
no one can see the kingdom of God unless he is born again."*
John 3:3

*Jesus answered, "I am the way and the truth and the life.
No one comes to the Father except through me."*
John 14:6

If we claim to be without sin, we deceive ourselves and the truth is not in us. If we confess our sins, He is faithful and just and will forgive us our sins and purify us from all unrighteousness.
1 John 1:8-9

If you confess with your mouth, "Jesus is Lord," and believe in your heart that God raised him from the dead, you will be saved.
Romans 10:9

*He (Jesus) himself bore our sins in his body on the tree,
so that we might die to sins and live for righteousness;
by his wounds you have been healed.*
1 Peter 2:24

For God so loved the world that He sent His one and only Son, that whoever believes in Him shall not perish but have eternal life.
John 3:16

Bible Verses

THAT ENCOURAGE US TO HAVE INSURANCE:

*A prudent man sees danger and takes refuge,
but the simple keep going and suffer for it.*
Proverbs 22:3

*The plans of the diligent lead to profit
as surely as haste leads to poverty.*
Proverbs 21:5

*Be sure you know the condition of your flocks,
give careful attention to your herds;
for riches do not endure forever.*
Proverbs 27:23-24

A good man leaves an inheritance for his children's children.
Proverbs 13:22a

*In the house of the wise are stores of choice food and oil,
but a foolish man devours all he has.*
Proverbs 21:20

*Do not boast about tomorrow,
for you do not know what a day may bring.*
Proverbs 27:1

*The rich rule over the poor,
and the borrower
is slave to the lender.*
Proverbs 22:7

BIBLE VERSES

*Go to the ant, you sluggard;
consider its ways and be wise!
It has no commander, no overseer or no ruler,
yet it stores its provisions in summer
and gathers its food at harvest.
How long will you lie there, you sluggard?
When will you get up from your sleep?
A little sleep, a little slumber,
a little folding of the hands to rest—
and poverty will come on you like a thief
and scarcity like an armed man.*
Proverbs 6:6-9

*A good name is more desirable than great riches:
to be esteemed is better than silver or gold.*
Proverbs 22:1

*Now listen, you who say,
"Today or tomorrow we will go to this or that city,
spend a year there, carry on business and make money."
Why, you do not even know
what will happen tomorrow.
What is your life?
You are a mist that appears
for a little while and then vanishes.
Instead, you ought to say,
"If it is the Lord's will
we will live and do this or that."
As it is, you boast in your arrogant schemes.
All such boasting is evil.
If anyone, then,
knows the good
they ought to do
and does not do it,
it is sin for them.*
James 4:13-17

CHAPTER 3

STAGE ONE: SHOCK

When something drastic happens that is too unbelievable for us to emotionally grasp, we encounter the first stage of grieving, which is known as shock. During the shock stage, we experience feelings of numbness, disbelief, and even denial, because our senses are too overwhelmed to accept our circumstances.

Since we cannot handle all of the implications of the tragedy at once, our bodies equip us to manage these situations by allowing us to go into the shock stage, which serves as a form of resilience when faced with calamity. According to Westberg (2012), "When the sorrow is overwhelming, we are sometimes temporarily anesthetized in response to a tragic experience. We are grateful for this temporary anesthesia, for it keeps us from having to face grim reality all at once" (p. 32). We are more likely to experience shock when the event happens suddenly and unexpectedly, and is far beyond our control.

This explains why, if we have ever witnessed a traumatic situation, such as a serious automobile accident, many times we find that rather than expressing deep emotions, the victims are moving about in a seemingly foggy state. They may struggle to comprehend what is happening or what is said to them. They are probably experiencing the shock stage.

The amount of time we remain in this stage depends on many factors, such as the nature of our loss, our psychological makeup, and how much our loss will impact our lives. The more unexpected and catastrophic our loss, the more time we may spend in this stage. If our loss comes "out of the blue," catching us completely by surprise, then we are likely to struggle for a while to grasp the reality of the circumstances. If a loved one dies after an extended illness, or a job loss comes after years of an employer's financial struggles, we may move more quickly through this stage. However, if a person remains in shock for several weeks, "it probably is unhealthy grief and professional help ought to be sought" (Westberg, 2012, p. 32).

While this stage protects the victims from experiencing all of the deep emotions at once, it can be misleading to family and friends. Due to the victims' initial lack of emotion, we may mistakenly think they are not sad over the loss, or their faith is so strong they will not grieve, or worse, they did not really love the person or thing they lost. We may conclude that due to their strong faith or emotional stability, they are fine, and do not need any help. Do not dismiss them just yet. They are probably still in shock, and have a long way to go.

The way to help a person out of this stage is to do the exact opposite of what we may think is helpful: allow the person to do as much as possible for himself. According to Westberg (2012), this is crucial:

> It is good for [the grieving person] to keep fairly busy and continue to carry on as much of our usual activities as possible during the period of crisis. It is certainly not good to have someone take over completely for us at such a time and make all the decisions for us. Well-meaning relatives and friends might hinder the grief process by forcing us to sit inactively by (p. 34).

The challenge for those who want to help during this stage is to determine what the person can and cannot do for him/herself. I witnessed this while my family and I were waiting in the hospital emergency room when my Uncle Richard was experiencing chest pains. While he was being examined, several of us mentioned to our Aunt Paula that she should eat lunch. She agreed, but, understandably, did not want to leave his side. Lunch was brought up a couple of other times, but no one took action. I realized she was in shock and we would have to decide for her, so we appointed someone to go to a nearby deli to get her lunch. Out of politeness, she protested, but we ignored her protests since this was an obvious need and someone had to create a plan to fill this need. When we inquired about what sandwich she wanted to order, she simply could not decide. She could only tell us the foods she did not care for, and then we ordered for her. When the food came, she accepted and ate it gratefully. Later, she again thanked us, adding that due to the hectic activities of the day, she forgot to eat dinner, and was thankful she had consumed a good lunch. While it is important and therapeutic to allow victims to do as much as possible in order to help them through this stage of shock, it is also necessary to use discernment to determine what they can and cannot do.

There is no time limit for being in shock, and even after people appear to move out of this stage, it is still normal for them to wrestle with accepting the reality of the situation in the ensuing days and months. While intellectually a person may accept their situation, it may take longer for them to accept it emotionally. This is typical and to be expected (Westberg 2012, p. 36).

> We are more likely to experience shock when the event happens suddenly and unexpectedly…

Journal Entries

July 1, 1991

Life between the accident and the funeral was like navigating through a dense fog. Life after the funeral is surreal. Our out of town guests return home, and family and friends go back to work. They revert back to their normal lives, but nothing is normal for me now. When everyone was in town for the funeral, they were a distraction, and consequently a postponement of the painful grieving process. As they leave, the emptiness begins to settle in. I am forced to face the reality of my situation.

Returning to everyday activities without Gary is a difficult adjustment, but God eases me back gently. Due to my injuries, I am unable to do the most basic things by myself, such as walk without assistance, much less take care of my daughters. I need to rely on others for everything. This brings challenges, but the blessing in this is that I am not yet left alone. My mother is staying with me for the first week and my older sister, Cyndi, who lives out-of-state, will stay with me for the rest of the summer. She has already been taking care of the girls and established their routine.

Other family members are also struggling with the loss, but I am so self-absorbed I cannot reach out to any of them.

Practical Advice for the Shock Stage

FOR THOSE WHO ARE GRIEVING:

1. Go easy on yourself. Do not put any additional pressure on yourself right now. Your concentration is at an all-time low. You cannot expect to be very productive. Do what you can do, but then lean on others for the rest. Try to take some time off work and limit your normal activities. If you must resume work, try to start back slowly, perhaps reducing the amount of hours that you put in. This is really not a good time for you to take on any important or intricate projects. A good goal may be to try to get back into your routine. Ask others to extend some grace to you at this time.

2. Accept help. Allow others to help you do the things you cannot do. People want to help you, but don't know how. You may feel shy about asking for assistance, but wouldn't you do the same for them in their time of need? Do not try to do everything yourself. Do the things you must do, and then communicate your needs to others who are willing to help you.

Practical Advice for the Shock Stage

FOR FAMILY AND FRIENDS OF THOSE GRIEVING:

1. Don't take over. Let grieving people do as much as possible for themselves. It's natural to want to step in and perform tasks for hurting people, but in order for them to move on with their grieving, they need to do as much as they can for themselves. Balance is the key here. It may be helpful for them to have you nearby, ready to assist them with whatever they cannot do.

2. Be sensitive. Check on them often, and try to be mindful of their needs. If they need their space, give it to them. Do not take this personally. If they want company, try to be there for them. Needs will vary depending on their personality and the nature of their loss.

3. Follow up. Casually double-check their work at this point. Don't criticize and don't belittle them, but if they are, for instance, cooking, you might want to make sure they turned off the oven, or put the milk back into the refrigerator instead of in the cupboard. Just keep an eye on them.

4. Bring food. Dropping off a meal is still a good idea at this point. People who grieve may either cut down on their eating or overindulge.

If they are eating less than they should, try to encourage them to eat something, especially healthy foods. If they are overeating, though, now is probably not the best time to point it out.

5. Offer assistance. Some everyday events may just be too hard right now, like getting the children to school on time, walking the dog, or running errands. If you see that some things are being neglected or they are really overwhelmed with some responsibilities right now, you may want to offer your assistance to help ease their burden. My sister-in-law used to do my grocery shopping for me. I'd give her money and a list, going over every item with her. Then she would purchase my groceries while she shopped for herself. This was a huge help to me, saving me from having to hobble through the grocery store on my crutches.

> While intellectually a person may accept their situation, it may take longer for them to accept it emotionally.

Bible Verses

TO COMFORT DURING THE SHOCK STAGE:

The righteous cry out, and the LORD hears them;
He delivers them from all their troubles.
The LORD is close to the brokenhearted
and saves those who are crushed in spirit.
Psalm 34:17-18

Be merciful to me, LORD, for I am faint;
O LORD, heal me, for my bones are in agony.
My soul is in anguish. How long, O LORD, how long?
Turn, O LORD, and deliver me;
save me because of your unfailing love.
Psalm 6:2-4

The LORD is my light and my salvation—whom shall I fear?
The LORD is the stronghold of my life—of whom shall I be afraid?
When evil men advance against me to devour my flesh,
when my enemies and my foes attack me, they will stumble and fall.
Though an army besiege me, my heart will not fear;
though war break out against me, even then will I be confident.
One thing I ask of the LORD, this is what I seek:
that I may dwell in the house of the LORD all the days of my life,
to gaze upon the beauty of the LORD
and to seek him in his temple.
For in the day of trouble
He will keep me safe
in His dwelling;
He will hide me
in the shelter of
His tabernacle
and set me high upon a rock.
Psalm 27:1-5

The LORD is a refuge for the oppressed,
a stronghold in times of trouble.
Those who know your name will trust in you,
for you, LORD, have never forsaken those who seek you.
Psalm 9:9-10

The Spirit of the Sovereign LORD is on me,
because the LORD has anointed me
to proclaim good news to the poor.
He has sent me to bind up the brokenhearted,
to proclaim freedom for the captives
and release from darkness for the prisoners,
to proclaim the year of the LORD's favor
and the day of vengeance of our God,
to comfort all who mourn,
and provide for those who grieve in Zion—
to bestow on them a crown of beauty instead of ashes,
the oil of joy instead of mourning,
and a garment of praise instead of a spirit of despair.
They will be called oaks of righteousness,
a planting of the LORD for the display of his splendor.
Isaiah 61:1-3

BIBLE VERSES

> When we feel the urge to cry,
> we should allow ourselves
> to weep until the tears stop.

CHAPTER 4

STAGE TWO: EMOTION

When the shock wears off and we start to grasp the depth of our loss, we may begin to experience the Emotion Stage. During this stage we make a radical change from the emotionless "Shock" stage. Instead of feeling numb and detached from our emotions, we begin expressing our feelings by crying frequently and sometimes uncontrollably. We may feel tremendously distraught and like we are falling apart (Harrison, 1992, p. 683).

Regardless of gender or age, everyone should feel the need to cry at some point during the grief process, and depending on the nature of our loss and our psychological makeup, we might cry a great deal. This is not bad, and we should not feel that we must apologize for this.

As uncomfortable as this may be, it is vitally important to cry and get our emotions out during this stage. As Westberg (2012) states,

> Sometimes without warning there wells up within us an uncontrollable urge to express our grief. And this is exactly what we ought to do: allow ourselves to express the emotions we actually feel. We have been given tear glands, and we are supposed to use them when we have good reason to use them (p. 32).

The Bible records several instances of people weeping due to their grief. Hannah wept in the temple when she could not have a child (1 Samuel 1). When David and his men came back to his town and found that his camp had been burned and his wives and children taken captive, he and his men wept (1 Samuel 30). In Genesis 50, we find Joseph, the second in command over the country of Egypt, weeping and throwing himself upon the body of his father, Jacob, who had just passed away. He was joined in his grief by all of the Egyptians who mourned over Jacob's death for seventy days. Even Jesus wept over the death of his friend, Lazarus, in John 11.

We do not have a record of these people ever apologizing for their tears, and we should not feel the need to do this, either. It is actually unhealthy to suppress our tears. When we feel the urge to cry we should allow ourselves to weep until the tears stop. If we are too embarrassed to cry in front of others, then we should go off somewhere to be alone and grieve (Westberg, 2012, p. 34).

Captain Richard Phillips was the merchant marine captain of the ship, *The Maersk Alabama*, who was captured by Somali pirates and held hostage in a life boat for several days in 2009. He experienced this type of emotional release after he was rescued in a daring mission executed by the U.S. Navy and U.S. Navy Seals. The first morning after he was rescued he woke up out of a deep sleep at 5:00 a.m., bawling his eyes out. He was embarrassed by this, realizing he had not cried like that since he was a boy. He forced himself to stop crying. The next morning he woke up the same way. When the SEAL team leader asked how Captain Phillip's was sleeping, Captain Phillips sheepishly shared what he was experiencing. The SEAL team leader insisted that Captain Phillips speak with the SEAL psychiatrist. Captain Phillips was surprised when the psychiatrist guessed that he was having episodes of crying. The psychiatrist explained that this was normal and told him the next time he started crying not to stop it, but let it run its course. The next morning when Captain Phillips was awakened by his crying at 5:00am he let himself cry. "For 30 minutes, tears streamed down my face and I didn't try to stop them. Waves of sadness and grief washed over me. And I let them. It was the strangest feeling. And it never came back," (Phillips, 2013, p. 274).

The amount and frequency of crying depends on the nature of the loss and the personality of the person. Some people will cry more than others, but everyone should cry. Expressing our emotions is actually quite healthy. We should feel the freedom to cry when we are sad. When we have experienced a great loss, it is only normal to do so. Crying does not mean we are weak or that we do not have strong faith. It is a natural expression of our grief at this time.

Journal Entries

July 8, 1991

On Monday, nine days after the accident, I finally cry for the first (but certainly not the last) time. I am out of the hospital, almost everyone else has gone back to their regular routine, and I am left alone with my grief. Someone has wisely bought several boxes of tissues and deposited them all over my house. I am starting to go through them.

My Mom is a huge help to me, and consequently at the end of the week when she prepares to return home, I fall apart. Another loss. It is hard on her, too, to leave me.

Someone suggests I go to a Christian counselor to deal with my grief. We set up the appointment, and I begin weekly sessions with a wonderful counselor. For the first several sessions all I do is cry.

Life becomes a cycle of follow-up doctor visits, counseling sessions, crying.

My church members are wonderful. They anticipate my every need and fill it. Since our only car was totaled in the accident, I do not have a vehicle and had not even thought about replacing it. One church member had a connection with a local car dealer, and arranged for me to borrow a used car, free of charge. Since this seemed to be an open-ended agreement and I did not want to take advantage of them, I offered to just buy it from them until I figured out what car I wanted to buy to replace the Mustang.

Cyndi agrees to stay with us over the summer and help me get acclimated to my new circumstances. I am no fun to be around and probably making her life miserable, like mine. Yet the Holy Spirit works through this situation and she becomes a Christian when a relative shares the Gospel with her; definitely no thanks to me.

In light of the major tragedy we are dealing with, it would seem that I would appreciate every little thing, realizing how short life is. Yet, ironically, the smallest things begin to annoy me, like the way friends fold my laundry. And they are doing me a favor!

Some people ask me if I'm angry at the driver or at God, and I tell them "no," because I know this is God's will. [This will change dramatically later.]

My mental capacities suffer (vanish?) after the funeral, especially my short-term memory. I ask a question, and then do not comprehend the answer, nor do I remember asking it, so then I ask the same question again. People often have to say things to me three or four times before I understand. Also, I cannot seem to have a cohesive thought; I keep jumping around from subject to subject.

When I am stressed, I tend to eat more than usual. But I discover that when I am traumatized, my appetite diminishes.

The finality of my situation sets in, and I realize I have a long, miserable road in front of me. I am afraid that it will be a long time until I feel happy. Will I ever feel joyful again?

When I go to church, I feel like everyone is watching me. I want to be a good witness to others right now in the midst of this trial. I want people to know that I have not turned away from God, and I will continue to come to church on Sundays and worship God. Fortunately, my family members have been coming with me and sitting with me, so

JOURNAL ENTRIES

I am not alone.

The week after the funeral, I had to meet with the police so they could finish their report on the accident. They said I could wait until I felt better, but I wanted to get it over with. I was fairly useless because, thankfully, I still do not remember any of the accident. I did ask the officer what the color of the vehicle that hit us was. I was surprised to find out that it was a dark blue Ford Ranger pickup with a camper, because that's what I have been picturing in my mind! However, it was upside-down at the scene, and the mental image I have of it has the truck upright.

From the police, I learned more details of the accident. Apparently, the driver had been coming from a child's birthday party at a nearby county park when he ran the stale red stoplight at the intersection we were crossing. It is believed that he had been drinking beer all day long and was extremely inebriated by this time. Witnesses said he showed no sign of stopping. His truck broadsided our car, and then flipped over us, coming to rest upside down.

There are articles in the paper about the accident. I am shown one, but kept from seeing another one that has a picture of our wrecked car. I am fine with not seeing it. How will it help me to view that?

Another thing I wanted to do immediately was clear out my husband's things. Some people find it comforting to keep their loved one's items around. But to me it only brings pain; a constant reminder that he is no longer here. While cleaning out his closet, Eddie [my husband's cousin and one of his best friends] stopped by. I gave him some of Gary's personal items. I also separated some of Gary's things for other family members, and some I kept for myself and the girls.

I thought it might help comfort his relatives to have some of his personal things as mementos. It was a difficult task, and tears were shed (what else is new), but it had been hanging over my head, so I felt relieved when it was finished.

My counselor warned me that little things might catch me off guard and bring me down, such as picking up a roll of film from being developed, and finding pictures of Gary, which happened. It is a bittersweet moment; I am happy to see pictures of him, but it is another reminder of the life we had together.

A little over two weeks after the accident is our first holiday without Gary—4th of July. Fortunately, it is a minor holiday in our family. Relatives invited us to their house for a cook-out, and I wanted to go. Maybe this won't be so bad, I told myself. I dressed the girls and myself in red, white, and blue, trying to be festive. We arrived at their house to find a group of about twenty caring family members and close friends. At first I did okay, but Gary's presence was sorely missed. My stomach began to get that empty feeling, that feeling that something is critically wrong and will never be right again. After dinner, I retreated to the bathroom, where I broke down and cried. Christy came in to check on me and I told her that I just cannot do this. I did not want others to see me crying and draw attention to myself, or ruin everyone else's fun. She and my mom helped plot my escape and we excused ourselves from joining the group to see fireworks and returned back to my house instead. Once home, I did not want to leave, so my family graciously stayed with me, and we caught just a glimpse of some fireworks from my front yard. I was glad when the holiday was finally over.

JOURNAL ENTRIES

Later, I learned that my in-laws also had struggled with the holiday. I was not alone in my gloom, yet I did not share it with others for fear I would bring them down.

Before Gary's death, I never understood why some people dread holidays. To me, they meant traditions, gatherings, fun, festivity, friends, and family. But when an important element is missing from this picture, it magnifies your pain. Now I can understand why many people feel apprehensive about holidays and even go so far as to commit suicide during the Christmas season.

My counselor thinks that it is good that I am still on crutches, because it is a reminder to others that I am still grieving. I can see how there was value in wearing black clothing or black armbands while grieving for someone in the past. Too often people forget that we are grieving and expect people to "get back to normal" quickly, not realizing how long the process can take.

I woke up one morning after having a wonderful dream about Gary, and for a split second I thought everything was normal, and then it hit me that Gary had died, and nothing was normal anymore, and it STINKS.

July 10, 1991

As part of my counseling, I'm supposed to write in my journal what is most difficult for me during this adjustment. The worst is seeing my daughters suffer. Laurel misses her Daddy so much and can't understand why he's gone or why he won't come back (much less that he's not ever coming back). This past Saturday Greg stopped by. When he left, she started screaming for her Daddy.

Lindsay has been very cranky, probably due to all of the changes. It doesn't help either of us that I can't even pick her up or hold her right now. She's at the stage where she only likes to be held by someone standing up, which I still can't do physically.

JOURNAL ENTRIES

The paperwork also has been a burden. Filing insurance claims, filing for Social Security Survivor's benefits, and taking care of the hospital bills, not to mention our normal expenses, has been overwhelming. Gary has always taken care of our personal matters, much to my relief. Thankfully, his parents have been helping me.

Also, thinking of the future without my companion and best friend is devastating. I can only think of short term things right now–the long term is too overwhelming.

July 12, 1991

I met with my counselor again today, and she revealed to me that I am trying to be strong for everyone else and live up to the expectations of others. I am not allowing myself to cry like I should. She informed me that I need to go through the natural grieving period or it will hit later. Consequently, I cried a lot today.

We were at the mall a couple of days ago and Karin decided to look for a shirt to give to Greg for his birthday. I thought it would be a good idea for me to pick out one for him, too, but when we walked in the Men's Department, I was suddenly overwhelmed with a sense of sorrow. It hit me that I used to shop here for Gary and now I can no longer do that. I thought I might burst out crying. I was caught off guard—another jolt of my new, horrible reality.

JOURNAL ENTRIES

July 17, 1991

Today I had another counseling session. Counseling gives me security. It makes me think I'm on the road to recovery.

My counselor revealed to me that I'm not allowing myself to deal with this. It's true, I can distract myself, because, frankly, who wants to deal with this? It is painful. She said self-pity is okay at this point. She also thinks I'm learning from this experience so that hopefully I'll be understanding and empathetic to someone else in the same situation.

The hardest thing I did today (and all week, for that matter) was pick out Gary's marker for his grave. I did just what she said and I cried when I felt like it, instead of trying to choke back my tears for the sake of the others. The salesman met with a group of us at my in-law's house. It was nice of him to come to us, although, frankly, he could benefit from more compassion training and less sales training.

The hardest thing that I dealt with yesterday was grasping the reality of my situation. While reading my Bible, I came across Romans 7:2, which states that when the husband dies, you are no longer married. The Social Security forms that I filled out also had a space which you had to fill in the date the marriage ended. At 7:30 p.m. on Saturday, June 22, 1991, I was happily married, and by 10:00 p.m., without my consent and definitely against my desire, I was no longer married. It seems so unfair–I did not want my marriage to end.

Gary would not be proud of me right now, because I have no idea how much money is in my checking account. That has always been work for me, to stay up on my finances. Anything that was challenging for me before the accident is now almost impossible. He always insisted that I know my balance. I hate to talk about him in the past tense; it's just one more reminder that he's gone.

I have some new fears now. I am afraid that I will be left out of "couples" gatherings because I am no longer one. I want people to know that I still count, even though there is only one of me. Maybe they think if I was included that it would hurt me too much, and maybe they are right.

July 27, 1991

This has been a very rough week. My counselor said it's because the shock is wearing off and the emotional part is kicking in. She said you can't force it; it just happens.

I received a call that Gary's grave marker was going to be set in place, so Karin and I decided to meet them at the grave site. At first we did okay, which shocked me, actually, but then we both started bawling.

"I never thought we would have to do this at this point in our lives," she said. I agree.

I spend a lot of time in self-pity, knowing God is sovereign, but still questioning why this had to happen.

The drunk driver's wife sent me a nice sympathy card with a personal note saying words could not express how sorry she feels. That was nice. I do not blame her, and I feel badly for her. Now she is a widow, too, although her husband was an irresponsible idiot. At least at Gary's funeral I could hold my head up. How do you bury your husband, when you know that he died due to his irresponsibility, and

JOURNAL ENTRIES

not only destroyed his own life, but he destroyed another family as well?

I've been very interested in what heaven will be like and what Gary's doing now. I've read all of the passages in my Bible about heaven. I was also gleaning every fact I could from near-death experiences, but then a wise friend warned me to be cautious with these, and compare everything to the Bible. If the account disagrees with the Bible, then I should be skeptical of it.

My counselor said it is normal to feel selfish at this stage of grieving. Good to know I am normal. She encourages me to go through the stages naturally and not try to ignore them or put them off. If I refuse to deal with the stages of grieving, I might deal with them later in the form of bitterness. As difficult as all of this is to deal with, I certainly do not want that. I am praying that I will go through each stage and not become bitter.

God seems to be far away from me lately. My mother-in-law said she feels the same way. Many people told me that when they went through a difficult time, they felt closer to God than ever. I do not feel this way; in fact, I feel just the opposite. I feel like God had me in the palm of His hands before the accident, but then He just dropped me and let me free fall.

> My counseling sessions and books on grieving helped me to understand that the emotions I was experiencing were normal.

Practical Advice for the Emotion Stage

FOR THOSE WHO ARE GRIEVING:

1. Read the Bible. Let me encourage you to get in God's Word. It is important to stay close to Him now; you need Him! The Psalms or the Gospel of John might be a good place to start.

2. Spend time in prayer. You may not feel like it, but this, too, is important in order to stay connected to God. Your prayers do not need to be elaborate; remember, God already knows your needs.

3. Pray God's promises. When you find a verse that deals with your situation, turn that verse into a prayer. God is faithful to His promises to us, but we need to know what they are. After Gary died, I discovered Psalm 68:5 ("A Father to the fatherless, a defender of widows is God in His holy dwelling"), and I have prayed this verse every day since then, asking God to fill the gap missing in my daughters' lives due to the loss of their father. And who could be a better father to them than our perfect, omniscient, omnipresent, omnipotent heavenly Father?

4. Take short field trips. As tempting as it is, I recommend you do not isolate yourself right now. Short trips to the store or outside are helpful. Fresh air and a change of environment can be very therapeutic now.

5. Attend church. You probably feel down, and perhaps you are afraid you will cry in church. It is still important to go and worship corporately. Again, I encourage you to seek God at this time. You also need the fellowship of a church family. If it is too difficult for you to get to church, or you do not want to walk in alone, see if someone will pick you up or meet you there. It would also probably be very helpful to be part of a Bible study, especially a small group of caring individuals. This will allow you to focus on God's Word and fellowship with other believers. These may be two great goals for you right now.

6. Keep a journal. Keeping a journal can be a therapeutic way to process all of the disjointed thoughts that may be spinning around in your head right now. I recommend you buy a journal or create a document on your computer to record your thoughts. Writing in it daily is helpful, especially in the beginning. If you cannot do it daily, write in it as often as needed.

PRACTICAL ADVICE

7. Stock up on tissues. Kleenex boxes are a good investment for you at the moment. Get several boxes and distribute them all over your house, car, work, and any other areas where you spend a lot of time. Allow yourself time to grieve and cry.

8. Get couseling. Grief is very difficult to wade through, much less alone. There are many counseling options. Depending on the nature of your loss, you may want to meet with your minister. He may meet with you once or twice to help you discuss your situation. If you need more extensive help, you can join a support group or see a counselor or therapist. You could check with your church to see if they have any groups or they may be able to recommend a private counselor. You can also check on the internet. I strongly recommend a Christian counselor. You may need to attend weekly counseling sessions at first, and then you will "graduate" to every other week, once a month, and so on. If the first counselor does not work out, it does not mean that counseling is not for you. Please try others. Your insurance may pay for all or part of it. Counseling and books on grieving helped me to see that the emotions I was experiencing were normal.

9. Read "Job" in the Bible. There is probably no one in the Bible who lost more than Job did, and yet he kept his faith throughout his trials. He still hurt badly and wrestled with many emotions, but he never turned from God. I recommend reading the introduction of the book, then chapters 1-3, which relate Job's losses, followed by chapters 38-42, in which God speaks to Job.

10. Arrange for diversions. Movies and television can be good short-term diversions at this time. However, you may want to avoid stories that have a plot similar to your circumstances so as not to accentuate your loss. I enjoyed renting comedies. They allowed me to temporarily escape my circumstances and sometimes even made me laugh.

11. Create a memento. If you are dealing with the loss of a loved one this may be helpful for you. My counselor suggested that I turn my husband's wedding band into a memento to remind me of him. I had a jeweler convert it into a "family ring" by mounting each one of our birth stones on it. I found it comforting to wear. Perhaps you have a piece of jewelry from your loved one that you can turn into a ring, necklace, key chain, or some other personal item.

12. Learn about Heaven. If you have recently lost a loved one, you may thirst for more detailed information about heaven during this time. One word of caution: if you hear about a near-death experience, compare the facts to the Bible. If the account disagrees with the Bible, be cautious about believing it.

Practical Advice for the Emotion Stage

FOR FAMILY AND FRIENDS OF THOSE GRIEVING:

1. Share your talent. Now that the initial shock has passed, there may be a great deal of needs. My church members, family, friends and neighbors took care of almost all of my needs. This taught me that one person cannot meet all of someone's needs, but many people can use their individual talents to help in some way.

2. Encourage spiritual self-care. Grieving people need to be strengthened in their faith right now. You may want to offer to take them to church. Help them stay accountable by asking them if they are spending time praying and reading their Bible every day.

3. Pray for them. They may not feel close to God at the moment, and may have a hard time praying themselves. Perhaps you can pray for their healing, their faith, and any specific needs they have right now.

4. Provide a Bible. I have many Bibles at my house, but a group of four friends bought a nice, compact Bible, and each one took a turn highlighting her favorite verses. Then they gave me the Bible, and encouraged me to keep highlighting verses as I read through it, which I did. There were times that I was so deep in my grief that I could not pray or focus on one passage of Scripture, so I would open up that little Bible and flip through the pages, stopping at the highlighted verses. It was extremely encouraging to me. The verses they highlighted are included at the end of almost every chapter in this book.

5. Encourage them to journal. You could buy them a journal to help them get started with this healing step.

6. Meet urgent needs. After the accident, I did not have a car, but before I was released from the hospital, a friend of the family had already secured the use of a car for me. Try to evaluate the needs of those who are grieving, and determine what you can do to help them.

> PRACTICAL ADVICE

7. Provide meals. Different church members prepared and delivered dinner to my house every day for three months after the accident! This was a huge help. We probably would have eaten a lot of junk food otherwise.

8. Schedule a visit. A few people would call me up and ask if they could stop by. I found their visits encouraging. I appreciated when someone would call in advance and stay for just a short time (half an hour worked well for me). Some would even bring a small gift, such as baked goods, which we enjoyed.

9. Call, text, or email. Reaching out to someone struggling with a loss is helpful. The method you use depends on how technologically savvy the person is and what you feel comfortable doing. Several people called or left messages for me. Even if I was unable to take the call at the moment, I appreciated their kindness in reaching out to me.

10. Send a card. For weeks after the funeral, I continued to receive cards from friends and relatives. It meant a great deal to me to know that they still remembered me and the pain I was in. I was especially impressed with people who remembered the monthly anniversary of the accident, and realized that was a hard day for me. It is never too late to send a card.

11. Give a thoughtful gift. One friend, not knowing how to reach out, made a cassette tape (today that would be called a CD or a playlist) of Christian music for me to listen to. The uplifting, God-centered praise music brought comfort to me.

PRACTICAL ADVICE

12. Show hospitality. Some families felt led to invite us over to dinner. It was great for us to get out and enjoy the company of others.

13. Offer to drive. Since I was not able to drive for a while after my surgery, several people took me to my many follow-up doctor appointments. This enabled my sister to stay home and babysit my young daughters, instead of having to drive me and entertain them in the waiting room.

14. Offer to help clean. Another friend from church helped me clean my house every Monday. This motivated me to clean, and I would work with her. When I was having a bad day, she graciously let me rest and cleaned alone. (When I inquired about when she cleaned her house, she shyly admitted that she had a cleaning lady come do it.)

15. Offer to do yard work. A neighbor I had never even met heard about our accident. He owned a lawn service and just started cutting my yard, free of charge, because he knew I would be unable to do it. After a few months, my Bible study group offered to pay for the service for a year, and since I did not want to take advantage of my neighbor, they took over.

16. Help with maintenance. This can be especially helpful to elderly people and single mothers. Two men from my Bible study came over and worked on my sprinkler system, which had constantly been a problem, and, again, was something I could not maintain by myself. Even if a family can do a job, they may not be able to at this time, so an offer to help may really meet a need.

PRACTICAL ADVICE

17. Give financial advice. If this is your profession, financial advice may be needed at this time. Since this a confidential and sensitive area, not everyone can do this. A member of my church was a financial advisor, and he was able to help me formulate a plan for my new life as a single mom. My brother-in-law met with me weekly for a few months to help me go over my budget and finances. Even if this is not your area of expertise, you may be able to recommend someone who can help.

18. Ask a ministry to "adopt" them. I was very blessed by a "Youth Group Invasion." My church's high school youth group asked if they could do a "work day" at my house. I agreed, and one Saturday, about 25 teenagers and their leaders invaded my home. Their parked cars lined my street. They came in and literally did everything! They cleaned my attic, my garage, my house, my windows, and my cabinets; did yard work; washed my loaner car; played with my children—everything imaginable. They were awesome. Not only were they a huge help to me, but they were also a great testimony to my neighbors.

In addition to the previous suggestions of tangible ways you can reach out to others, here is some advice on how to show your support while interacting with them:

19. Do not give "pat" answers. Trite phrases, such as, "Everything will work out for the best" or "God is using this to make you stronger in your faith," will probably be perceived as heartless and annoying. You are not going to be able to "fix" someone's loss with such comments, especially if you have not endured anything similar to what they are going through.

20. Let them talk and cry. You may feel awkward and inept, but you really do not need to say much. Often just listening and being empathetic is incredibly helpful.

21. Do not depend on them. If you need them to do something for you, make sure it is something unimportant. For instance, if you invite them to dinner and they insist on bringing something, allow them to bring something that you can live without, in case they forget or have to cancel at the last minute.

22. Be patient with them. They may have a difficult time remembering things that you told them.

23. Understand anniversaries. The monthly anniversary of the loss and every holiday for the first year will most likely be very difficult. Also, the loved one's birthday and wedding anniversaries can be very painful. To this day, it means so much to me when people say, "I know this is a hard day for you. How are you doing?"

24. Be sensitive to their changes. If your friend recently had a miscarriage, for example, being around other women who are pregnant is probably going to be hard for her. Try to consider what upcoming events might be difficult for grieving people, and prepare them for or shield them from these things.

> **PRACTICAL ADVICE**

25. Don't offer any advice now. Just be empathetic. Now is not the time to point out their errors. In the Bible Job's friends made the mistake of doing this. Job was a righteous man who God allowed Satan to test by taking Job's wealth, his children, and his health. Job's friends graciously came to comfort him, but instead of consoling him, they tried to figure out what he did wrong to deserve the suffering God allowed Satan to inflict on him. In addition to Job's mental and physical anguish, he now had to argue with his friends and defend himself. Don't put your grieving friend or relative in that position. Listen and be empathetic now. After the crisis passes there may be time to discuss why this situation happened.

Bible Verses

TO COMFORT DURING THE EMOTION STAGE:

A father to the fatherless, a defender of widows,
is God in His holy dwelling.
Psalm 68:5

He [God] will wipe every tear from their eyes.
There will be no more death or mourning or crying
or pain for the old order of things has passed away
[in the new heaven and the new earth, from Rev. 21:1].
Revelation 21:4

As the deer pants for streams of water,
so my soul pants for you, O God.
My soul thirsts for God, for the living God.
When can I go and meet with God?
My tears have been my food day and night,
while men say to me all day long, "Where is your God?"
These things I remember as I pour out my soul:
how I used to go with the multitude,
leading the procession to the house of God,
with shouts of joy and thanksgiving among the festive throng.
Why are you downcast, O my soul? Why so disturbed within me?
Put your hope in God, for I will yet praise him,
my Savior and my God.
Psalm 42:1-5

I wait for the LORD,
my whole being waits,
and in his word I put my hope.
Psalm 130:5

I am worn out from groaning;
all night long I flood my bed with weeping
and drench my couch with tears.
My eyes grow weak with sorrow;
they fail because of all my foes.
Away from me, all you who do evil,
for the LORD has heard my weeping.
The LORD has heard my cry for mercy;
the LORD accepts my prayer.
Psalm 6:6-9

Listen to my words, LORD, consider my lament.
Hear my cry for help, my King and my God, for to you I pray.
In the morning, LORD, you hear my voice;
in the morning I lay my requests before you and wait expectantly. For
you are not a God who is pleased with wickedness;
with You, evil people are not welcome.
Psalm 5:1-4

Yet the LORD longs to be gracious to you;
therefore he will rise up
to show you compassion.
For the LORD is a God of justice.
Blessed are all who wait for him!
People of Zion, who live in Jerusalem,
you will weep no more.
How gracious he will be when you cry for help!
As soon as he hears, he will answer you.
Isaiah 30:18-19

BIBLE VERSES

> Grief has become our constant companion—a parasite we cannot shake off.

CHAPTER 5

STAGE THREE: DEPRESSION AND LONELINESS

After a while, we begin to feel depressed and lonely. According to Byron (2007), "It is estimated that around 30 per cent of bereaved people are also depressed one month after the loss, with 15 per cent being depressed a year later."

The support of friends and family may have waned. Perhaps we think we should be feeling better by now, but we may actually feel worse. We have now experienced several situations with our altered status, and we do not like it. Grief has become our constant companion—a parasite we cannot shake off. We are sick of feeling terrible, but we do not see any end in sight. It may seem like it is going to be a long time before we feel better. During this time it is common to feel like we are moving laboriously through life with a huge boulder on our back.

We may feel alone and as if no one has ever felt like we do now. Since everyone deals with loss differently, no one has felt exactly like we do. However, others have felt isolated and utterly depressed during their grieving. When this despair sets in we should remember that after a significant loss it is normal to feel this way (Westberg, 2012, p. 36).

We may also feel that God is far away from us. This, too, is not uncommon. In the Bible David cried out to God in the Psalms, "Why have you forgotten me?" On the cross Jesus cried out, "My God, my God, why have you forsaken me?" According to Westberg (2012),

"When we are depressed, we find ourselves thinking thoughts we never have otherwise. We say God does not care. We may even doubt that there is a God" (p.39).

One valuable lesson I learned during my grieving is that faith should not be based on feelings. Although I did not "feel" close to God, He demonstrated His love for me through the countless acts of kindness that His people showed me during my grieving. We get into danger when we base our faith on our emotions. Just because we do not "feel" God, does that mean that He does not exist? Is God's existence based on my feelings? I hope not! We cannot depend on our emotions, especially right now. We can, however, depend on the Bible, which tells us of God's love, His faithfulness, and His promises to us.

We can also depend on the third member of the Trinity, the Holy Spirit. God has promised never to leave us or forsake us (Hebrews 13:5), and one way He accomplishes this is by having the Holy Spirit reside in believers. The Holy Spirit helps us in many ways. He is our Comforter, Counselor, Helper, Intercessor, and Advocate. He is the Spirit of Truth (John 14:16-18, 26-27) Who strengthens us and stands by us in crisis.

It is important to realize that it is natural to have feelings of doubt and depression during this time. More importantly, though, we need to realize that we will not always feel this way. This is a temporary state.

Before my husband's death, I could never understand how someone could commit suicide. Now I can. I am not saying I want to commit suicide, because I do not. However, there were times during my grieving when I felt so low that I can now understand how people become so desperate that they feel ending their lives is the only way to end their pain. Other common escapes we might try to turn to right now are addictions, such as alcohol, drugs, over-eating, pornography, or anything else we think will alleviate this depression. The problem with addictions is they only provide a temporary escape, but can have very negative consequences. Also, the guilt, loss of self-respect, and lack of self-control we may feel after participating in these self-destructive behaviors will only make us feel worse, not better.

The important thing we MUST realize during this stage is that we are not always going to feel this way. Better days will come, although they may not arrive as quickly as we would like. When we are in a state of depression, it is difficult, and sometimes even impossible, to realize that the heaviness which has descended upon us will pass. But it will pass. We will not always feel this way. Better times will come.

Also, we must remind ourselves that God has a plan for our lives and our suffering is part of His plan. No one is immune to suffering. In John 16:33 Jesus tells us, "In this world you will have trouble. But take heart! I have overcome the world." God can and will use our suffering for good, although it may take a long time for us to realize what that good is. I know he did that with my loss. Through Gary's death, both my sister and my grandmother came to know the Lord as their personal Savior. However, sometimes during my depression this knowledge was not enough to comfort me.

I also experienced this type of depression and doubt while I was out of work after losing my job. I sought God and He brought me a better job. After assuming my new position, I quickly began learning new skills, making more money, and feeling happier. I realized that I would never have left my previous job without God's prodding. If He had not moved me out of my former place of employment, I would have missed out on the many blessings of my new one. God is working through these circumstances, and although we do not understand it now, it is important to trust Him during this difficult time.

God also teaches us valuable lessons during our low times. He used my misery during my depression to teach me a great deal about myself—things that would not have been revealed to me through my normal, everyday activities. For instance, God revealed that I had been very proud of my husband's career accomplishments in the field of aviation and the perks we enjoyed as a result. It was humbling to see how much value I had put into that.

Remember: God has left us here on Earth for a reason. We need to trust Him, desperately cling to Him, and expect Him to be faithful to His promises during this time.

We also need to examine our attitude during this stage. During our period of depression, we may find we have become pessimistic. Although we ought to focus on the positive, it may be tremendously difficult for us to do so right now. This may make us hard to love. It has been my observation that the hardest people to love are often the ones who need love the most.

However, the feelings of isolation and depression will pass. For some people, the depression passes suddenly. They experience a revelation that liberates them from this state, never to return again. Others, though, myself included, find it to be a process of "one step forward and two steps back." We progress, but do so painfully and slowly. The important thing, though, is we are making progress, and this is what we need to focus on.

If we find ourselves steeped in depression for an extended period of time then we may be experiencing clinical depression, which means we need to get professional help to pull out of it. If we are having suicidal thoughts we need to tell our doctor, relative or close friend IMMEDIATELY. There are options, such as counseling and medication, that can help us overcome this deeper depression. We may be able to progress normally through this stage, but if it becomes overbearing, we should ask for help.

Journal Entries

July 20, 1991

Anything that was a challenge before the accident now seems impossible for me. For instance, before the accident, I was bad about returning calls. Now I am terrible at it. Several people call and leave messages on my answering machine. I listen to their messages and think, "Oh, that is so nice of them," but I rarely return their calls. It is just too much effort.

I've noticed an interesting thing about my friends at this time. Some old ones drop off, while new ones surface. Some people keep their distance. Others, however, and God bless them, feel led to reach out and seem to know how to handle the situations, despite how difficult I am.

Julie came over today and relieved my older sister from watching the girls. Every time she comes over she helps me accomplish something. Today we cleaned out the refrigerator. It does not seem like a big deal, but lately everything is a big deal. I have very little motivation, and most tasks seem overwhelming, so I just procrastinate most of the time. I am grateful for her initiative and her help, because I do feel better when these jobs are accomplished.

I went to Bible Study tonight, the same group we were going to when we had the accident. They were all wonderful! I was so glad that even though I'm no longer a "couple," they are including me.

July 22, 1991

Yesterday was a horrible day. It seemed like everything was coming down on me. We went to church, ate lunch at one relative's house, and then stopped to visit other relatives. It went okay, but everyone was tired, so the day kind of dragged. Being tired makes things worse. I felt like I would cry at any moment and even started once.

Then the drive home was probably my worst hour so far. It was the waning evening hours when you still could go outside and do something. This particular time of the week has never been easy for me. I used to always feel lonely at this time when Gary was out of town. Now it is just magnified. I could not wait to get home and let my sister handle the girls while I excused myself and went to my bedroom and just cried. I bawled for an hour. When I finally finished crying, I read from my Bible, which comforted me. Then my brother Jimmy called me and we talked, which was helpful. What a rough day!

Today was better, except I was mean to Cyndi most of the day. She went tattling to my mom that I'd been told by my friends at Bible Study that I was conscious at the scene of the accident. This was news to me because I don't remember any of it, thankfully, but apparently I had conversations with the police officers and paramedics. When she got off the phone, I blew up at her. I told her to quit trying to censor my life. Why do they think I would be better off not knowing that I was conscious at the scene of the accident? I can't stand it when they try to hide things from me, like when they hid Gary's Bible from me because they thought I would be upset if I saw it. Meanwhile, I was going out of my mind looking for it. That really angers me! I felt better after blowing off steam, but of course she did not. I was still mean the rest of the day.

JOURNAL ENTRIES

July 29, 1991

Greg's birthday is in two days, and Karin thought it would be nice to throw him a surprise party. No one really feels like partying, but she thought it would be good for everyone to have something fun and positive to do.

Forgetting my limitations, I agreed to help, although, frankly, I do not feel like it. Everything is an effort right now. I keep thinking I can do everything, like before the accident, but I cannot.

After I spend time at home, I get antsy and I want to go out. But when I go out I realize I don't like to be in public for very long, and then I want to return to my sanctuary–my own home.

July 31, 1991

Last night I told Cyndi to "take a night off." The poor girl has been with me non-stop, and I'm sure she needs a break. The girls and I ate dinner, played and then I put them down and paid my bills at the kitchen table. It felt good to be a little productive.

Unfortunately, as I was getting ready for bed, I saw a man on my lawn, walking up to my bedroom window. I hobbled to the kitchen on my crutches and called 911, and while I was on the phone, he tried to break into my living room sliding glass door. I was terrified. It seemed to take forever for the police to come. I could see the minutes ticking away on the digital clock on the VCR. I thought he would be successful and come inside before the police got anywhere near my house. The police finally came and saw him, but he got away.

The police, like the dispatcher, seemed pretty heartless. They had me write my name on a piece of paper (not sure why, but nothing makes

JOURNAL ENTRIES

sense to me right now) and it looked like a five-year-old's signature, it was so shaky and uneven.

Despite the apathy of the policemen, Frieda [my neighbor] came right over. She was comforting. Cyndi came home while the police were still here, and she felt horrible for leaving me alone, but, of course, it wasn't her fault!

After the police left, I called my Uncle Al, who was a sheriff in the next county. He kindly staked out my house in the community pool parking lot, which was across the street from my side yard.

No one really slept well last night. I got out of bed this morning, but I am useless. I felt like I was almost coping with grieving but I feel like I'm over the edge now. Gary's death was horrible enough; now this. I just recently thought to myself, "God doesn't give you more than you can handle, so certainly I'm at that point now and nothing worse will happen," and now this does. I was wrong. I feel completely depleted.

Mid-morning one of our ministers stopped by to visit. He had no knowledge of the events of the previous night, so I filled him in from the chair that I was slumped in. After he left, he called Keith and Lori [friends from church who were our neighbors] and they stopped by to offer support and comfort. I do not know what to tell them; I can't even think straight. But, again, their efforts to reach out to me are extremely comforting.

Tonight we are supposed to throw Greg's party. Ha! I can't do anything. I was supposed to cook part of the meal. Now we settle for me picking up a six-foot sub, and I wonder why I thought I could do even that much. I felt like a robot at the party; everything is a blur. I did not feel very festive.

JOURNAL ENTRIES

August 4, 1991

After the intruder tried to break in, different family members took turns spending the night on my couch, because we were too shaken up to stay alone. Finally we had an alarm system installed, which allows me to sleep, but I still feel a little paranoid, wondering if this guy will come back, since the police never caught him. I don't like the fact that he tried to do this the first night I was alone. Has he been watching me? I have also decided to put a large fence around my backyard, which would have been needed eventually for safety reasons due to the little lake that is behind my house.

September 10, 1991

My mother-in-law thought it might be helpful to enroll Laurel into our church's pre-school two mornings a week. But I cannot get motivated in the mornings. Thankfully God has provided the help I need. On the mornings Laurel goes to pre-school, Karin comes over before she goes to work and helps get Laurel ready. I can hardly get out of bed and sometimes I don't until she rings the doorbell, I am ashamed to say. But she does not make me feel guilty. She gets the girls up, turns on some lively music, and while dancing and playing with them, she gets them both dressed and fed. I only have to get myself ready, and I can hardly do that. By the time she leaves, all I have to do is strap them in their car seats and head to preschool. What a blessing she is!

Last week, I was feeling particularly low. I felt like God had forgotten me. Then the phone rang. I could not even answer it because I had been crying, so I let the answering machine take it. It was our youth pastor, Dale Goodman, who was in charge of the "youth group invasion" work day at my house shortly after the accident. He said, "Hey Tammy, I just wanted to check on you and see if you need anything. The youth group is able to come out to your house and do another cleaning day if you want us to. I know it's been a few months since Gary died. If you need anything, we are here for you. We just wanted to let you know that we have not forgotten you." I was amazed at the timing of his call, and especially his last sentence! I am encouraged and humbled to think that God answered me, just when I needed it most.

JOURNAL ENTRIES

At first, it was so important for me to still be recognized among other couples. I was afraid of being left out and of any changes in my social life. Now sometimes it is just easier to be left out of couples' events, rather than go and highlight my singleness.

I've also noticed a change in my attitude over the past few months. After Gary died, I appreciated lots of help and intervention; for instance, others helping discipline my children. Now, however, I am annoyed by it; it seems more like interference.

I also notice that I am very negative, like when some other mothers recently invited me and my daughters to join them on a trip to a local animal park, all I could see was it was dirty and run-down.

I feel like there's a cloud on my shoulder, and I want it to lift, but I feel like it never ever will. I shared this with sister-in-law and she said she feels the same.

Everything is such an effort now—it's like having the flu. I just am not motivated to do anything. I feel a heaviness in my heart and my future seems bleak. It seems like this will never end.

I have gotten into a bad cycle lately. I get out of bed at the very last

> **JOURNAL ENTRIES**

minute on the mornings that Laurel does not have preschool, often leaving my girls in their room too long after they awaken. When they take their afternoon nap, I often take one, too. I'm tired; everything is an effort. Plus, going to sleep is an escape from my reality. Unfortunately, since I often get a good two-hour nap, I'm not tired when it is time to go to bed. Consequently, I stay up too late. And it's not like I'm being productive. I do not feel like doing anything, so I just watch late night television or do other unproductive stuff. Maybe part of this has to do with not wanting to go to sleep in an empty bed.

November 16, 1991

My days have been very empty and lonely lately. I thought I was making progress, but now I seem to have regressed. Why can't my husband be here with me? I miss him so much. I can't stand it when other women complain about their spouses. I think, you don't know how stupid you are! You should appreciate your wonderful husband. I guess I should take my own advice and appreciate what I still do have. It's just so hard because I have known a better life that I no longer have. I just had the girls' pictures taken professionally. Lindsay would not smile for anything. The photographer was a bozo, but I was trying to be patient with him. He said he had not seen anything like her. I thought, how would you feel if you lost your Dad just four months ago? I wonder if she is a mirror image of me. She does smile around her family, though.

    I wish I could hug Gary again. This STINKS! I need him now more than ever, as I go through the worst thing in my whole life, and he is not here for me.

> When we are in a state of depression, it is difficult, and sometimes even impossible, to realize that the heaviness which has descended upon us will pass.

Practical Advice for the Depression and Loneliness Stage

FOR THOSE WHO ARE GRIEVING:

Take Care of the Basics!

1. Get enough sleep. Being tired only makes things more difficult to handle. If you have bad habits, such as not being able to sleep at night because you are taking long naps during the day, try to reverse your body's schedule. If you are having trouble getting to sleep, you might try some tactics to relax your body before bedtime, such as taking a bath, reading a book or drinking a tea designed to help you sleep. You might also want to try a natural supplement or over-the-counter sleeping pills.

2. Eat, and eat healthy food. Be sure to eat during this difficult time. Know your body. How does your body react to caffeine, artificial sweeteners, sugar, junk food, and other unhealthy items that we eat? Caffeine and artificial sweeteners might make you edgy. Sugar will provide an energy burst, but it is followed by a crash. Consider your diet. Have any of these foods been affecting you negatively? Try to eat healthy foods and drink plenty of water.

3. Exercise daily. Make it your goal to do so. Exercise releases endorphins in the brain, which contribute to the feeling of happiness. If you have exercised in the past, you may not feel up to the level of intensity you are accustomed to. Do not feel pressured to work at a high level. Just getting outside and walking or riding a bike for twenty minutes can help clear your brain and give you a better perspective.

4. Get fresh air. Be sure to go outside and try to enjoy nature. Take deep breaths and feel the sunshine. If you have been stuck inside and depressed, it may help to get a new perspective.

5. Consider antidepressants. Prescription drugs are not for everyone, but your counselor and/or doctor can determine if you should take an antidepressant. We all want the pain to go away quickly. A pill will not do that for you, but it might take the edge off. One warning, though: some antidepressants have the opposite effect and can actually make you feel worse, not better. If you are taking an antidepressant and you are still feeling depressed, or even worse than you were before taking the medication, talk to your doctor about trying a different one. There are several different brands and it may take some experimentation (medically supervised, of course) to find the right one for your body.

6. Arrange a trip. You may feel that you need a change of scenery by now. This might be a good opportunity to get away for a few days. Plan wisely. Give yourself enough privacy and freedom in your schedule to be able to go to your own room and cry if you feel the need. You might consider taking someone with you. You may find it therapeutic to go to a different part of the country and try some new, yet non-stressful activities. If someone has invited you to visit and you think it would be a healthy environment for you, accept their hospitality and go.

7. Be selectively social. You may dread going to certain social events now. Every social event may not be right for you at the moment, but do not miss out on all of them because you feel awkward. Arrange to ride or meet up with others before you go to a social event. Give yourself the freedom to leave early if you are uncomfortable. Look for others who are in a similar situation, and reach out to them.

8. Assess your security. If you are alone now, consider getting an alarm system for your house. Not only will it go off if someone tries to intrude, but the alarm panel also warns you if it has gone off while you are out.

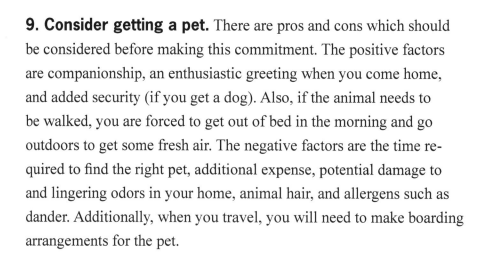

PRACTICAL ADVICE

9. Consider getting a pet. There are pros and cons which should be considered before making this commitment. The positive factors are companionship, an enthusiastic greeting when you come home, and added security (if you get a dog). Also, if the animal needs to be walked, you are forced to get out of bed in the morning and go outdoors to get some fresh air. The negative factors are the time required to find the right pet, additional expense, potential damage to and lingering odors in your home, animal hair, and allergens such as dander. Additionally, when you travel, you will need to make boarding arrangements for the pet.

> Just getting outside and walking...
> can help clear your brain
> and give you a better perspective.

Practical Advice for the Depression and Loneliness Stage

FOR FAMILY AND FRIENDS OF THOSE GRIEVING:

1. Give encouragement. Encourage those who are grieving to get enough sleep, eat well, and exercise. If they say they are struggling in one of these areas, offer to help by bringing them some healthy food or exercising with them.

2. Keep bringing food. Those grieving may not feel like cooking, and a nourishing meal is both helpful and appreciated.

3. Offer to help with travel. You may offer to accompany those who are grieving on a trip, or if you live out of town, offer to have them come to visit you.

4. Help assess their security. If they need an alarm, fence, or another item for safety, you could suggest it, and offer to help them find the right devices and/or installers.

5. Get approval before you get a pet. A pet can be a wonderful friend for grieving people, but do not get them one without their consent; such a move has potential for disaster. If you think they would benefit from one, discuss it with them.

6. Watch them closely. If they seem to be descending into deep depression they may not be able to help themselves and need assistance in getting help. Be aware of signs of suicide. Refer to the information provided by Suicide Awareness Voices of Education (2014, "Symptoms and Danger Signs," para. 1-2):

Warning Signs of Suicide

These signs may mean someone is at risk for suicide. Risk is greater if a behavior is new or has increased and if it seems related to a painful event, loss or change.

- Talking about wanting to die or to kill oneself.
- Looking for a way to kill oneself, such as searching online or buying a gun.
- Talking about feeling hopeless or having no reason to live.
- Talking about being a burden to others.
- Talking about feeling trapped or in unbearable pain.
- Increasing the use of alcohol or drugs.
- Acting anxious or agitated; behaving recklessly.
- Sleeping too little or too much.
- Withdrawn or feeling isolated.
- Showing rage or talking about seeking revenge.
- Displaying extreme mood swings.

Additional Warning Signs of Suicide

- Preoccupation with death.
- Suddenly happier, calmer.
- Loss of interest in things one cares about.
- Visiting or calling people to say goodbye.
- Making arrangements; setting one's affairs in order.
- Giving things away, such as prized possessions.

> PRACTICAL ADVICE

> *A suicidal person urgently needs to see a doctor or mental health professional.*

Bible Verses

TO COMFORT DURING THE DEPRESSION AND LONELINESS STAGE:

How long, O LORD? Will you forget me forever?
How long will you hide your face from me?
How long must I wrestle with my thoughts
and every day have sorrow in my heart?
How long will my enemy triumph over me?
Look on me and answer, O LORD my God.
Psalm 13:1-3

But now, this is what the LORD says—
he who created you, O Jacob,
he who formed you, O Israel:
"Fear not, for I have redeemed you;
I have summoned you by name; you are mine.
When you pass through the waters, I will be with you;
and when you pass through the rivers,
they will not sweep over you.
When you walk through the fire, you will not be burned;
the flames will not set you ablaze.
For I am the LORD, your God,
the Holy One of Israel, your Savior;
I give Egypt for your ransom, Cush and Seba in your stead.
Since you are precious in my sight, and because I love you,
I will give men
in exchange for you,
and people in exchange
for your life.
Do not be afraid,
for I am with you.
Isaiah 43:1-5

Though you have made me see troubles,
many and bitter, you will restore my life again;
from the depths of the earth you will again bring me up.
You will increase my honor and comfort me once again.
Psalm 71:20-21

Hear me, LORD, and answer me, for I am poor and needy.
Guard my life, for I am faithful to You; save your servant who trusts in you. You are my God; have mercy on me.
Lord, for I call to you all day long. Bring joy to your servant, Lord, for I put my trust in you. You, Lord, are forgiving and good, abounding in love to all who call to you. Hear my prayer, LORD; listen to my cry for mercy. When I am in distress, I call to you, because you answer me.
Psalm 86:1-7

If you say, "The LORD is my refuge,"
and make the most high your dwelling, no harm will overtake you, no disaster will come near your tent.
For He will command His angels to guard you in all your ways; they will lift you up in their hands
so that you will not strike your foot against a stone.
You will tread on the lion and the cobra;
you will trample the great lion and the serpent.
"Because he loves me," says the LORD,"
"I will rescue him; I will protect him,
for he acknowledges my name. He will call on me
and I will answer him; I will be with him in trouble,
I will deliver him and honor him.
With long life I will satisfy him and show him my salvation.
Psalm 91:9-16

BIBLE VERSES

I consider that
our present sufferings
are not worth
comparing with the glory that will be revealed in us.
Romans 8:18

> Our emotional well-being *does* affect our physical health.

CHAPTER 6

STAGE FOUR: PHYSICAL SYMPTOMS OF DISTRESS

Not only do we experience emotional turmoil during grieving, but we may also exhibit physical symptoms of distress. This is a normal part of the process. We may experience new physical ailments at this time, such as dizziness, pain, stomach problems, or headaches. Alternatively, we may encounter a recurrence of a previous medical problem. For instance, if we have suffered from migraines in the past, we are likely to be vulnerable to these headaches now. These may be signs of grieving or an actual illness. It is important to seek medical attention to determine the cause of the problem and the proper course of treatment.

Not only might we encounter health problems during our initial grieving period, but we may also experience them later as a result of not working through the grief process. According to Westberg (2012),

> As a clergyman in a medical center, where I have worked closely with doctors and their patients for many years, I have slowly become aware of the fact that many of the patients I see are ill because of some unresolved grief situation. Usually the patient first went to see the doctor with a physical complaint. In an increasing number of cases these people tell me about some great loss they have sustained during the past months or year or two. As we talk, it is clear they have not yet worked through some of the cen-

> tral problems related to that loss. I see this so often that I cannot help drawing the conclusion that there is a stronger relationship than we have ever thought between illness and the way in which a person handles a great loss (p.42).

Our emotional well-being does affect our physical health. For this reason, we must work through our grief. If we stall, the emotional pain will not go away. Rather, it will come out through some other avenue in our life, quite possibly through physical malaise. For both our emotional and physical health we must deal with our grief, as unpleasant as the process may seem.

> Not only might we encounter health problems during our initial grieving period, but we may also experience them later as a result of not working through the grief process.

Journal Entries

August 2, 1991

I cannot understand why now, weeks after the accident, I am experiencing some different medical problems. I am intermittently experiencing dizzy spells, stomach aches and headaches. I am concerned about these. Is there something else wrong with me from the accident that my doctors missed? Am I having complications from my injuries? I had one of my many follow-up doctor appointments today, so during this visit, I described my new symptoms to my doctor. Then I even had a dizzy spell in his presence, which I was thankful for, so he could actually see what I am talking about. Upon further examination, he determined that the only cause of these ailments was stress. He said I did not need any medicine; they will dissipate over time. I felt like a hypochondriac, since there is no medical cause for them. But when I thought about it later, I remembered that when I was a child, my stomach would act up during stressful times in my life, like when my parents went through their divorce. I guess I should have expected that. However, the dizziness is new. Thankfully I know what it is, and I don't need any medicine or further tests.

February 17, 1992

Dinners can be stressful, because it is difficult to try to eat and feed my girls at the same time, especially if they are whiny. Eating this past weekend was problematic because my stomach was upset. I had indigestion and it felt like I had rocks in it. I had to medicate it and eat only bland food. If I talked about or thought about something even mildly controversial, it would flare up. Fortunately, after a few days, it improved.

Practical Advice for Physical Symptoms of Distress Stage

FOR THOSE WHO ARE GRIEVING:

1. Seek medical attention. If you experience problems with your health during this time, have a physician check them out. Do not just assume that these issues are a result of your grief and will go away in time, or that you do not need to see a doctor. The symptoms may be signs of something serious. Also, whether or not your symptoms are due to your loss, your doctor may be able to prescribe treatment to help. Let your doctor diagnose you.

2. Assess your diet, exercise, and sleeping patterns. Any medical issues you are experiencing may be due to not eating well, not getting enough exercise, or not getting enough sleep. You may need to modify your routine to reduce your physical symptoms of distress.

Practical Advice for Physical Symptoms of Distress Stage

FOR FAMILY AND FRIENDS OF THOSE GRIEVING:

1. Encourage your loved ones to seek medical attention. If people who are grieving have physical problems, take their symptoms seriously. They will not know the cause unless they consult a doctor. Encourage them to seek medical help. You may want to remind them that it would be better to know for certain if their symptoms are a sign of a medical condition that needs treatment.

PRACTICAL ADVICE

2. Help assess basic physical needs. If your friend is complaining about physical symptoms of distress, you may question them about their current diet, exercise, and sleeping patterns. Encourage them to focus on any of these areas which need improvement.

> Assess your diet, exercise and sleeping patterns... You may need to modify your routine to reduce your physical symptoms of distress.

Bible Verses

TO COMFORT DURING THE PHYSICAL SYMPTOMS OF DISTRESS STAGE:

Do not be wise in your own eyes; fear the LORD and shun evil.
This will bring health to your body and nourishment to your bones.
Proverbs 3:7-8

A cheerful look brings joy to the heart,
and good news gives health to the bones.
Proverbs 15:30

Is any one of you in trouble? He should pray.
Is anyone happy? Let him sing songs of praise.
Is any one of you sick?
He should call the elders of the church to pray over him
and anoint him with oil in the name of the Lord.
And the prayer offered in faith will make the sick person well; the Lord
will raise him up. If he has sinned, he will be forgiven.
Therefore confess your sins to each other and
pray for each other so that you may be healed.
The prayer of a righteous man is powerful and effective.
James 5:13-16

A cheerful heart is good medicine,
but a crushed spirit dries up the bones.
Proverbs 17:22

Hope deferred
makes the heart sick,
but a longing fulfilled
is a tree of life.
Proverbs 13:12

> As a result of this preoccupation with our loss, we may find that our relationships, jobs, and any other activities that we are involved in suffer at this time.

CHAPTER 7

STAGE FIVE: CONSUMED WITH LOSS

During this stage we find that the majority of our thoughts are focused on the circumstances of our bereavement, resulting in an inability to concentrate. Because we are consumed with our loss and unable to think of anything else, this impacts our ability to focus, causing our concentration to suffer tremendously.

Not only are we consumed with our loss, but we may also become anxious as a result. We try to distract ourselves, which may work for a brief period of time, but soon we find ourselves thinking about our loss again. This naturally hinders us from being effective in anything we attempt to do (Westberg, 2012, p. 52).

As a result of this preoccupation with our loss, we may find that our relationships, jobs, and any other activities that we are involved in suffer at this time. Because our loss is permeating most of our thoughts, it is not a good time to take on any extra responsibilities. We may find we cannot even complete or enjoy our normal activities. Perhaps something we usually take pleasure in, such as a hobby or sport, is now something we perform well below our ability level or avoid altogether. This is to be expected. When we are unhappy, other areas of our lives are naturally going to suffer.

Not only are we unable to focus on the events of our daily lives, but we may be unable to focus on other activities, such as watching movies or reading. If you had to read this paragraph more than once to comprehend what is written, you may be experiencing this!

According to Westberg (2012),

> It is natural to be unable to concentrate during this point in our grieving. It would be more unusual if we were to perform our routine activities. When something which was extremely important to us has been taken from us we cannot help but be constantly drawn to the lost object. And we suffer daily as we struggle with the gradually dawning realization that it is gone forever, (p. 54).

We should not panic at this point. Take comfort in knowing that this is normal. We may also have unusual thoughts at this time. This is not a permanent state. If we continue to work through our grief, then we will come out of this.

One way to improve our situation is to focus on new and different things and relationships. It is easier to wallow in our grief and to hide at home, but it is helpful at this stage to venture out and meet new people or learn about new interests. This helps us take our minds off of our loss. Remaining in our gloomy state will only serve to prolong our grieving (Westberg, 2012, p. 56).

Journal Entries

November 14, 1991

At the last minute, I was invited to dinner tonight. I was able to find a babysitter, so I went, and it felt great to get out. Sometimes last-minute invitations are better for me. If my schedule is too full, I feel pressured and I want to cancel some of my commitments. However, if I do not have things to do, then I get edgy and want to get out. I am such a mess.

November 17, 1991

It still hurts so much—even more than it did in the beginning. I cannot believe that Gary is not here anymore. Is it just going to be getting harder and harder? I wish SO badly that Gary was here with me. I can't believe he is gone. The weekdays are not as bad because the girls and I had our little daily routine while he was at work. But the nights and weekends are difficult, because his absence is so obvious.

November 27, 1991

I seem to be doing better. I just watched a movie about someone whose life is far worse than mine. It makes me thankful for what I do have.

Tonight we went to dinner at the home of a family from church. We had a deep, honest talk about grieving. It is comforting to know other people miss Gary, too. Days like today give me hope.

JOURNAL ENTRIES

December 4, 1991

I have been back down in a slump lately. I feel so non-excitable. I'm dreading this Christmas, which stinks, because I have always loved this season. My counselor said I need to write down all of my feelings to get them out. She is trying to get me to accept that I am a single parent and going to be that way for a while.

Right now, I am sitting in front of our Christmas tree. It has been up for three days. We finally decorated it tonight. When I put on some Christmas music, I nearly cried, remembering how different things were last time I played those songs.

December 26, 1991

I hate not having Gary here. Christmas was very hard without him. On Christmas morning, I was holding myself together and not crying, until Pat [Julie's husband] gave everyone a framed copy of a poem he wrote about Gary. Of course everyone teared up. I broke down and cried and I did not want anyone to comfort me. I was mad at them, initially, for giving that gift that brought us all to tears, especially on such a hard day anyway, but now I am glad to have the poem—it is a good one.

My comprehension is very low lately. My brain seems so dull. I don't understand a lot of what I hear or read. This is normal, according to my counselor, and journaling will help it, so here I am.

Fortunately, I have had moments when I have felt happy, which I am grateful for.

February 5, 1992
A group of eighteen of us went skiing last week, including Christy, my daughters, and Coventry [their babysitter]. I was really looking forward to it. We skied well the first three days, but by the fourth day (our last day of skiing), I was missing Gary and unmotivated and depressed. I didn't ski well, as a result. I finally gave up and went into my room in the condo and cried. Other than that slump, we got along well and had a good time.

However, since I've been back, I have just been unmotivated. I have so much that I should be doing, but I cannot get myself to do anything.

February 13, 1992
Tomorrow is Valentine's Day. I have been trying to ignore it. Christy is being really sweet and taking me to dinner at one of my favorite restaurants, and then we are going to see a movie.

I am trying to decide whether to stay in our house or move. I have been praying about it and I am leaning toward moving. I was thinking about it the other day as I was in the backyard with the girls while they were playing on their swing set. I was watching them and I started crying, wondering how I could leave this home. It would be like dissolving my last link to my life with Gary. Then I just started thinking, he's not ever coming back. Of course, I know it, but there's just been some comfort knowing he used to live here with me. It would be so final to move. Moving in here had been such a joyous occasion. Our future held such promise then.

I was still crying and the girls started arguing when Aunt Holly [Gary's aunt] pulled up to visit. What timing, I thought. But I was just

JOURNAL ENTRIES

honest, telling her what I was going through. She felt badly for us, and invited us over for pizza, which was extremely kind. We went and had a great time.

I have not been very peaceful lately. I'm so tired, but I can't sleep. A million thoughts go through my mind. I feel as if there's a big void inside of me. Although I have things to look forward to, nothing makes me as happy as before, with Gary.

An observation I've made is that I crave food, but it doesn't ever taste as good as I thought it would. In fact, I find myself disappointed, because I thought it would be better than it was. But the lack of taste doesn't prevent me from eating; in fact, I have been overeating. I talked to my counselor about my lack of willpower. She said it doesn't seem to be hurting me, and since it is a minor issue in comparison to everything else I'm dealing with, not to worry about it at this time.

February 17, 1992

I am so tired. Christy shared her observation that people are starting to treat me like "normal" again by telling me their problems. What they don't realize is that I'm still suffering and not really able to help them yet.

I have been really close to tears lately. Also, I find that I am forgetful and distracted. I have to make a concerted effort to remember things. I find myself either thinking about the accident, or other major decisions. Sometimes I realize I have been ignoring my daughters, even if they are speaking to me.

March 26, 1992

Lately, I just feel empty. I don't feel depressed. I just feel like, what's the point? Of course, the point is my girls. I am in a horrible, exceedingly low valley in my life, and there's no quick or easy way out. That's what is so discouraging—knowing I'm not able to wake up tomorrow and everything will be all better. I also find it difficult to get motivated, even just to go to bed. I like to escape through movies, reading, sleeping, even daydreaming. They are better than facing reality.

Last night, after I put my girls to bed, I was feeling so low that I just sat down on my couch and cried. My neighbor knocked on the door, and since my car was in my driveway and she knew I was home, I had to answer it. It was embarrassing for me and she felt badly when she saw my tears. Tonight, she came over with Easter decorations and a plate of homemade cupcakes, surrounded by coconut dyed green to look like Easter grass. I was so touched! She works full-time and has a toddler of her own, yet she went to all of this trouble for us!

April 27, 1992

Today, I learned that Karen B's husband [my friend who helped me clean my house right after the accident] died suddenly last night. After some apprehension, I called her. I would say at this point that she's doing better than I am. She is in major shock. Making all of the funeral arrangements is keeping her busy. Fortunately, her family is here with her. She said they've been just wonderful, a great help. That will change, I thought to myself. In a few months, you will all be getting on each other's nerves.

JOURNAL ENTRIES

She said she thought a lot about me and about Gary's death before I called. I feel so badly for her. She has no idea of the awful days ahead of her. We are too damn young to be widows.

I had an appointment with my counselor today, who tried to get me to remember what I would have wanted someone to do to help me right after Gary died. Since I understand her loss as only a few people can, now is a very good time for me to be able to reach out to her and help her.

April 30, 1992

Joe's funeral [Karen B's husband] was the first one I have attended since Gary's, and it was exceedingly difficult for me. It was like reliving Gary's death all over again, except this time I was more alert and observant. I know most of the emotions that the family is dealing with, and I hurt for them. I keep making comparisons between the two. I didn't realize how difficult it would be for me to attend this (I never do—I never realize how hard these things will hit me).

I had no motivation this morning, so I just sat down and did my Bible study. It helped me immensely. We are studying Malachi, and the lesson dealt with bitterness toward God when His plans are not our plans, and we look around and see sinners prospering. It spoke to me. God has given me some hard, honest views of myself lately. It's very hard for me to forgive as Jesus does. And I still haven't forgiven the guy who took Gary's life, if I want to be honest.

I went to the Christian bookstore and bought my newly widowed friend a small Bible, a journal, and a copy of the grieving book that helped me.

June 21, 1992 (Father's Day)

JOURNAL ENTRIES

Today is Father's Day, and tomorrow is the one-year anniversary of the accident. It has been extremely rough. Last night, I went to Bible study, just like Gary and I had set out to do last year. I did not know if I could make it or not, but I went. The group was very considerate and even gave me a card.

This morning, I felt fine, just tired. We went to the early church service, which turned out to be much more difficult than I had imagined. I started crying so hard during the sermon that I needed the help of family members to get home. I was supposed to be a substitute in Laurel's Sunday School class after the service, but obviously I couldn't. (Why in the world did I volunteer to do that on this day, of all days?) Laurel started crying when I told her that I could not teach her class. Fortunately, Aunt Holly intervened and took over for me.

In the afternoon, we all went over to the community pool in my development, where we were having several family members over for lunch and swimming. By then, I felt better and even enjoyed playing in the pool with everyone. It was a relief to do something fun after such an intense morning.

Practical Advice for the Consumed with Loss Stage

FOR THOSE WHO ARE GRIEVING:

1. Seek new relationships/opportunities. Although it may be the last thing you may feel like doing, this could be helpful. You may want to take shelter at home and not deal with anything new right now, but branching out and doing different things will help you get past this stage.

2. Serve others. This may be a good time to start helping others. The most fulfilling thing we can do, paradoxically, is not to serve ourselves, but to serve others. It is time to realize that although what happened to you was awful, there are people who are suffering more than you are. It would be beneficial for you to get out there and help them, and start appreciating what you do have.

3. Choose your battles. If you currently have other issues (like my lack of self-control with eating), decide whether you want to tackle these now. If it is a health problem, then there is no question that it must be dealt with immediately. If, however, it is a minor issue (like you have gained ten pounds and really feel like you should be on a diet, but you find comfort in chocolate), perhaps you can deal with it when you feel better. Try not to invite any additional pressure or stress to your life right now.

4. Be thankful. Making a list of your blessings, perhaps in your journal, and thanking God for each and every one, whether big or small, is one way to do this. It may sound elementary, but it truly is helpful. Whatever we focus on will shape our thinking. Colossians 3:15-17 tells us,

> Let the peace of Christ rule in your hearts, since as members of one body you were called to peace. And be thankful. Let the word of Christ dwell in you richly as you teach and admonish one another with all wisdom, and as you sing psalms, hymns and spiritual songs with gratitude in your hearts to God. And whatever you do, whether in word or deed, do it all in the name of the Lord Jesus, giving thanks to God the Father through him.

PRACTICAL ADVICE

5. Censor your activities. Be selective about the movies and television you watch, as well as the books and magazines that you read. Try to avoid anything that will accentuate your loss.

Practical Advice for the Consumed with Loss Stage

FOR FAMILY AND FRIENDS OF THOSE GRIEVING:

1. Persevere in helping. Those grieving may be wearing you out with their situation by now. I encourage you to hang in there. They need friends now more than ever, although they may not act like it.

2. Arrange a "working" visit. If they cannot get motivated, arrange to work on a project with them on your next visit. Ask them if there is something they would like to do but have been putting off. My sister-in-law used to come over and help me do fairly easy projects that I just could not get motivated to do on my own. Being productive made me feel better. You could offer to use your talents to help those who are grieving feel productive also.

3. Create diversions. Help them find diversions, so they can get their mind off themselves. Movies, books, short trips, eating out, and helping others could all be good steps for those grieving right now.

4. Don't nag them. If they have developed or continued in some bad habits that are not life-threatening (such as overeating or overspending), don't nag them about these. Encourage them to work through their grief first, and later, when they are feeling better, they can focus on other problems.

> The most fulfilling thing we can do, paradoxically, is not to serve ourselves, but to serve others.

Bible Verses

TO COMFORT THOSE CONSUMED WITH LOSS:

When I said, "My foot is slipping," your love, O LORD, supported me.
When anxiety was great within me, your consolation brought joy to my soul.
Psalm 94:18-19

Why do you say, O Jacob, and complain, O Israel,
"My way is hidden from the LORD;
my cause is disregarded by my God?"
Do you not know? Have you not heard?
The LORD is the everlasting God,
the Creator of the ends of the earth.
He will not grow tired or weary,
and his understanding no one can fathom.
He gives strength to the weary
and increases the power of the weak.
Even youths grow tired and weary,
and young men stumble and fall;
but those who hope in the LORD will renew their strength.
They will soar on wings like eagles; they will run and not grow weary,
They will walk and not be faint.
Isaiah 40:27-31

BIBLE VERSES

I remain confident of this:
I will see the goodness
of the LORD in the
land of the living.
Wait for the LORD;
be strong and take heart
and wait for the LORD.
Psalm 27:13-14

*But Zion said, "The LORD has forsaken me,
the Lord has forgotten me."
"Can a mother forget the baby at her breast
and have no compassion on the child she has borne?
Though she may forget I will not forget you!
See, I have engraved you on the palms of my hands."*
Isaiah 49:14-16

*No king is saved by the size of his army;
no warrior escapes by his great strength.
But the eyes of the LORD are on those who fear Him,
on those whose hope is in His unfailing love,
to deliver them from death and keep them alive in famine.
We wait in hope for the LORD; He is our help and our shield.
In Him our hearts rejoice, for we trust in His holy name.
May Your unfailing love be with us, LORD,
even as we put our hope in You.*
Psalm 33:16-22

*Though the fig tree does not bud
and there are no grapes on the vines,
though the olive crop fails
and the fields produce no food,
though there are no sheep in the pen
and no cattle in the stalls,
yet I will rejoice
in the LORD,
I will be joyful
in God my Savior.*
Habakkuk 3:17-18

BIBLE VERSES

OTHER RECOMMENDED BIBLE VERSES:
Psalm 139:1-10

> If we have lost a loved one,
> we may regret things
> we did not do for this person
> when he or she was alive.

CHAPTER 8

STAGE SIX: GUILT

This stage may be experienced at any time during the grieving process. Some people feel guilt at the onset, while others do not experience it until later.

It is normal to have some feelings of guilt when we lose someone or something of value to us. If we have lost a job, our financial status, or a friendship, we may regret the words and actions that led to our loss. If we have lost a loved one, we may regret things we did not do for this person when he or she was alive. We may also experience feelings of guilt for things we have done that hurt the person. According to Westberg (2012):

> When we lose a loved one through death, it would be hard to conceive of any of us who had lived closely with the departed one who would not feel guilty about some of the things we did not do for this person when he or she was alive, or the things we did do that hurt this person. We know we have sinned against this person by thought, word, and deed and our religious training says we should face up to our sin, and we ought to feel guilty about it (p. 56).

Not only might we feel guilty for the way we treated them, but if they died, we may also feel guilty for their death, wondering if we could have done something to prevent it.

After my husband died, I felt extremely guilty. He had been working hard at two jobs all week, and he was weary and did not want to go out that night. I made him go. After his death I deeply regretted that I had coerced him to do this and I wondered if he would still be alive if I had not forced my way. Then, as I was reading my Bible, God graciously revealed to me Psalm 139:16, which states, "All the days ordained for me were written in your book before one of them came to be." What a precious verse! This freed me, because it tells us that before each one of us was even born, God had determined how many days we would live on earth. We have a finite amount of days to live here, and when it is our last day, no human can stop us. My husband did not die because of my selfishness. He died because it was part of God's plan. If we had not gone out that night, it still would have been his last day on this earth, and God would have taken his life some other way. Our heavenly Father is sovereign. If we believe this, then it makes sense that He alone controls everything, including the number of days that we are alive. He gives breath, and He takes it away. I hope this verse relieves you as much as it helped me.

Although we cannot always understand why things happen, we can trust God has a purpose. Romans 11:33-34 tells us, "Oh, the depth of the riches of the wisdom and knowledge of God! How unsearchable his judgments, and his paths beyond tracing out! Who has known the mind of the Lord?" God works through all of our situations, whether good or bad, for our ultimate benefit. Although we may not appreciate the circumstances, He can use them to teach us valuable lessons and to shape our character.

If we are suffering from guilt, we need to differentiate between normal guilt and neurotic guilt. When we do something we should not do, or fail to do something that we ought to do by society's standards, then we ought to feel normal guilt. Neurotic guilt, however, is feeling guilty out of proportion to our involvement in a problem. One challenge is that these two types of guilt are often intermingled, making it difficult to separate the two feelings (Westberg, 2012, p. 58)

Certainly, when the Holy Spirit convicts us of our sins, it is natural and beneficial for us to feel guilt that leads to repentance. Once we realize the actions of which we are guilty, we should confess our sins to God, and then let go of our guilt. God does not want us to remain in it. After we have confessed our sin and asked for God's forgiveness, then we need to trust His Word, which tells us over and over that we have been cleansed and forgiven. The Epistle 1 John 1:9 tells us, "If we confess our sins, He is faithful and just and will forgive us our sins, and purify us from all unrighteousness." (Actually, 1 John is a wonderful book of the Bible that discusses our sins and God's forgiveness. I encourage you to read it in its entirety.) We need to accept God's wonderful gift of forgiveness. Christ died to take our sins on the cross; we are not to take our sins back.

What should we do with our guilt? We should confess it, learn from it, and leave it at the cross. It's easier said than done, isn't it? When we feel ourselves taking it back, we should confess that to Jesus, and ask for His help in releasing us from it.

If we continue to feel excessively burdened, we should ask God to reveal to us whether or not we are suffering from neurotic guilt. If so, then we are taking on too much responsibility for things that are out of our control or do not involve us. We need to realize this and ask God to help us let it go.

Journal Entries

July 26, 1991

Some of my relatives have said that they do not want to know many details about the accident because they think it makes it harder to deal with. I found that they are 100% right. Now I feel strongly the same way. I just found out that the drunk driver had a drinking problem and his neighbor was not surprised to hear that he died from it. Then I started thinking, If this was such common knowledge, why did his family, friends, and neighbors allow him to continue in this destructive path? Why did they let him go to a social function, get drunk, and then try to drive himself home? These nagging questions do not help my healing one bit. I go back and forth between these earthly circumstances and what I know spiritually, like God is sovereign. Plus, they take me away from the truth, which is that God is in control and wanted Gary to go to heaven on that day. Psalm 139 has been a big comfort to me, especially verse 16, which tells that God knows how many days we were going to live before we were even born. God took Gary because it was Gary's time to die. I need to keep focusing on the eternal, not on the earthly circumstances.

August 8, 1991

There are so many things I wish had done differently for Gary. I wish I had taken better care of him, like when I found a pile of mending that I had been putting off. In it was a pair of pants he never got to wear because I had not made it a priority to hem them. I wish I had taken

JOURNAL ENTRIES

better care of myself for him; like, after my pregnancies, I should have tried harder to lose those extra pounds and dyed my hair back to blonde, even if the color came from a box since we couldn't afford for me to have a hairdresser do it. I wish I had not been so petty about stupid things. I wish I had not nagged him, I wish I had learned to communicate better with him, I wish I had not given him such a hard time about leaving me to go on "guy" trips with his friends. I wish we'd had more time together, and that he could've been here to see his daughters grow up, and been here to grow old with me, like we had planned.

Practical Advice for the Guilt Stage

FOR THOSE WHO ARE GRIEVING:

1. Confess to God. Confess both your normal and your neurotic guilt, and then let it go.

2. Forgive yourself. If God has forgiven us, then shouldn't we forgive ourselves? This is the only way to peace. If we trust that God is sovereign, then we realize that He has a purpose for everything.

3. Read 1 John. I recommend reading this New Testament Epistle. John, a close disciple of Jesus, writes a poignant letter on the assurance of our salvation in just five chapters.

Practical Advice for the Guilt Stage

FOR FAMILY AND FRIENDS OF THOSE GRIEVING:

1. Encourage forgiveness. Implore them to accept God's wonderful gift of forgiveness, reminding them that this is why Jesus died. For those who feel guilty over the loss of a loved one, share with them Psalm 139, which tells us that God determines everyone's date of death before he or she is born. Another great verse is Romans 8:28, which tells how God works through all circumstances for His glory and our good.

> PRACTICAL ADVICE

Bible Verses

TO COMFORT DURING THE GUILT STAGE:

For you created my inmost being;
you knit me together in my mother's womb.
I praise you because I am fearfully and wonderfully made;
your works are wonderful, I know that full well.
My frame was not hidden from you
when I was made in the secret place.
When I was woven together in the depths of the earth
your eyes saw my unformed body.
All the days ordained for me were written in your book
before one of them came to be.
Psalm 139:13-16

When Joseph's brothers saw that their father was dead, they said,
"What if Joseph holds a grudge against us and
pays us back for all the wrongs we did to him?"...
His brothers then came and threw themselves down before him.
"We are your slaves," they said.
But Joseph said to them, "Don't be afraid.
Am I in the place of God?
You intended to harm me, but God intended it for good
to accomplish what is now being done, the saving of many lives."
Genesis 50:15, 18-20

"This is the covenant I will make with them
after that time,"
says the Lord.
"I will put my laws
in their hearts,
and I will write them on their minds.
Their sins and lawless acts I will remember no more."
Hebrews 10:16-17

*For the director of music. A psalm of David.
When the prophet Nathan came to him
after David had committed adultery with Bathsheba.*

*Have mercy on me, O God,
according to your unfailing love;
according to your great compassion
blot out my transgressions.
Wash away all my iniquity
and cleanse me from my sin.
For I know my transgressions,
and my sin is always before you.
Against you, you only, have I sinned
and done what is evil in your sight,
so that you are proved right when you speak
and justified when you judge.
Surely I was sinful at birth,
sinful from the time my mother conceived me.
Surely you desire truth in the inner parts;
you teach me wisdom in the inmost place.
Cleanse me with hyssop, and I will be clean;
Wash me, and I will be whiter than snow.
Let me hear joy and gladness;
let the bones you have crushed rejoice.
Hide your face from my sins and blot out all my iniquity.
Create in me a pure heart, O God,
and renew a steadfast spirit within me.
Do not cast me from your presence
or take your Holy Spirit from me.
Restore to me
the joy of your salvation
and grant me
a willing spirit
to sustain me.*
Psalm 51:1-12

BIBLE VERSES

> *LORD, do not rebuke me in your anger*
> *or discipline me in your wrath. Your arrows have pierced me,*
> *and your hand has come down on me.*
> *Because of your wrath there is no health in my body;*
> *there is no soundness in my bones because of my sin.*
> *My guilt has overwhelmed me like a burden too heavy to bear.*
> *My wounds fester and are loathsome because of my sinful folly.*
> *I am bowed down and brought very low;*
> *all day long I go about mourning.*
> *My back is filled with searing pain; there is no health in my body.*
> *I am feeble and utterly crushed; I groan in anguish of heart.*
> *All my longings lie open before you, Lord;*
> *my sighing is not hidden from you. My heart pounds,*
> *my strength fails me; even the light has gone from my eyes.*
> *My friends and companions avoid me because of my wounds;*
> *my neighbors stay far away.*
> *Those who want to kill me set their traps,*
> *those who would harm me talk of my ruin;*
> *all day long they scheme and lie.*
> *I am like the deaf, who cannot hear, like the mute, who cannot speak;*
> *I have become like one who does not hear, whose mouth can offer no reply.*
> *LORD, I wait for you; you will answer, Lord my God.*
> *For I said, "Do not let them gloat*
> *or exalt themselves over me when my feet slip."*
> *For I am about to fall, and my pain is ever with me.*
> *I confess my iniquity; I am troubled by my sin.*
> *Many have become my enemies without cause;*
> *those who hate me without reason are numerous.*
> *Those who repay my good with evil*
> *lodge accusations*
> *against me, though I*
> *seek only to do what is good.*
> *LORD, do not forsake me;*
> *do not be far from me, my God*
> *Come quickly to help me, my Lord and my Savior.*
> Psalm 38:1-22

BIBLE VERSES

CHAPTER 9

STAGE SEVEN: ANGER AND RESENTMENT

Although none of the stages of grieving was enjoyable to go through, this was my least favorite. Some people encounter this stage immediately. For others, it may take quite a while. Most likely, though, it will come, and when it does it won't be any fun.

God created anger, and when used correctly, it does serve a purpose. There is righteous anger, and God expressed it often during the Old Testament, both toward the nations who were oppressing the Israelites, His chosen people, and toward the Israelites, when they strayed from Him and worshiped idols. In the New Testament, Jesus displayed righteous anger when He saw how the religious leaders of His day desecrated the temple by turning it into a market place (Matthew 21:12-17). Because He was protecting God's house, it was not a sin for Him to drive out the money changers and merchants.

However, much of the anger we experience during this stage of grieving is not righteous; instead, it is a normal, negative emotion. Every person experiences anger and resentment.

Most of us are unskilled in how to effectively handle our anger. This makes us uncomfortable with it, and consequently, desirous of suppressing it. This is neither healthy nor wise. We cannot bury it. When we find ourselves angry and resentful we should admit to ourselves that we are feeling this way, and then confess this to God and ask Him to help us overcome it. Harboring resentment is unhealthy, and it can take over and become very harmful. We must wrestle with it, and by the grace of God we can overcome it (Westberg, 2012, p. 61).

If we do not deal with anger, then it will resurface in our attitude in the form of bitterness. When we become bitter, others find it difficult to break through our negativism and embrace us as a friend. Trying to love someone who is bitter is like trying to hug a porcupine; it is difficult and painful.

We have all witnessed a person in public who has become disproportionally angry at an offense (or perceived offense) made against him. Perhaps he has verbally abused a waitress or cashier for a seemingly minor incident. The person who has unleashed this rampage is probably not that upset over the mistake, but is most likely venting on the poor, unsuspecting worker because of some uncontrollable situation in his life. Perhaps he has discovered that his spouse has been unfaithful, his child is on drugs, or a close relative has been diagnosed with a deadly disease. He is frustrated by these extenuating circumstances and lacks the proper communication skills to help him work through the anger in an appropriate manner, thereby causing him to explode over other minor situations. Perhaps we are that angry person. If we do not want to become this person (or continue to be this person), then we must work through our anger.

If we are honest with ourselves and realize that we have been the aggressor in these situations, we need to stop victimizing others. As Westberg (2012) wisely states,

> When we have something precious taken from us, we inevitably go through a stage when we are very critical of everything and everyone who was related to the loss. We spare no one in our systematic scrutiny of the event, attempting

to understand exactly why this thing happened, and who is to blame. The human is always looking for someone to blame. If we have lost someone through death, we express hostility toward anyone who cared for the patient. We are hostile to the doctor because he operated, or we are hostile to him because he did not operate. No matter what he did, it was wrong. While we are in this mood, we look at everyone with a jaundiced eye. If we talk to the minister and are encouraged to admit what we really think, one day we may say, "Why did God do this to me?" or "How can He be a God of love if He treats people like this?" With Thomas Carlyle we cynically say, "God sits in His heaven and does nothing" (p. 61).

In order to deal with our anger we have to dig it up and get it out in a therapeutic way. We need to find a way to physically release our anger without harming ourselves or someone else. There are several different ways to do this. When you are alone (and I recommend you do this while you are alone so no one thinks you are crazy) determine the best way to get out your anger, such as hitting a punching bag with boxing gloves, hitting a mattress with a racquet, doing Tae Bo, shooting basketball hoops, practicing your tennis serve, or another physical activity. Whatever you do you will not want to worry about accuracy (such as getting your tennis serve into the serving box). You may want to talk (or yell) during this time, and you may experience some tears while doing this (which is why you do not want an audience). All of these expressions of anger are okay. You should spend about 20 minutes doing this activity to fully get your anger out. Unfortunately, you are not always able to do this when the anger flares up. However, my counselor told me to start hitting my bed with a racquetball racquet, even if I did not feel anger at that moment. At first I started doing this sheepishly, feeling quite stupid and embarrassed about the whole ordeal. However, as I was hitting the bed the anger started to rise to the surface. After 20 minutes of dealing with this I was physically and emotionally exhausted, but it was therapeutic because I was able to release a lot of my anger through this exercise, and no one was injured during the process.

Our goal should not be simply to get our anger out. In order to heal fully we need to forgive. This is not easy or natural to do, but it can be done. Let's look at the circumstances surrounding forgiveness.

Who we need to forgive depends on our situation. Are we blaming ourselves? Others? God? In order to work through our grieving we need to get to the place of forgiveness. Forgiveness brings us freedom and peace. Lack of forgiveness keeps us in bondage. If we fail to forgive, who do we hurt? Ultimately, ourselves. Have you ever witnessed (or experienced) this? One person holds a grudge and is eaten up inside by it, while the person they hold a grudge against moves forward in life and experiences peace. Failing to forgive will harm us more than anyone else, because it will increase our resentment and make us bitter.

Why should we forgive? We need to realize what the Bible says about forgiveness:

- God commands forgiveness. If we have accepted Jesus as our Savior, then God has forgiven each of us of every single one of our sins through the blood of Jesus, which He shed on the cross for our sins. Several verses in the Bible tell us to forgive others, such as Luke 6:37, "Do not judge, and you will not be judged. Do not condemn, and you will not be condemned. Forgive, and you will be forgiven."

• Romans 8:28 reminds us, "And we know that in all things God works for the good of those who love him, who have been called according to His purpose." Even the evil things that happen are done for a purpose. We need to trust that God is working and that He can use these negative circumstances for our good and His glory.

• God's amazing forgiveness for us and His expectation that we forgive others is illustrated in "The Parable of the Unmerciful Servant," found in Matthew 18:23-35. A king has mercy on a servant and forgives him of a large debt of money that he will never be able to repay. The servant thanks the king but then orders a friend who owed him a small amount of money to be thrown into prison because he could not repay his debt. When the king found out about the servant's ingratitude, the king reinstated his debt and had him thrown into prison until the servant could repay the full amount. This is a warning to us that since God has forgiven us of many sins, large and small, we should forgive others.

How do we forgive? Here are some steps, portions of which were taken from Dr. Charles Stanley's article, "13 Steps to Forgiving the Unforgiveable," which was taken from his book, *The Gift of Forgiveness*. I recommend you follow these steps to confess your anger:

1. Understand that forgiveness does not mean that you are:
   a. denying you were hurt
   b. justifying or minimizing the behavior that the other person did to you
   c. explaining why the person acted this way toward you
   d. forgetting what happened

2. Realize forgiveness is a choice. You have to determine to forgive. Even if you do not feel 100% that you are able to forgive at this point, if you are willing to forgive and you follow these practical steps, then the feelings will follow.

3. Choose a time when you can be alone for a period of time to focus on this process.

4. Understand it is often beneficial not to forgive the person face to face. If the person is unavailable or unaware of your intense feelings of anger, it is probably better not to confront them.

5. Start with prayer.
   a. Confess to God your anger and resentment toward the person who offended you.
   b. Ask the Holy Spirit to remind you of all of the

people you need to forgive and all of their transgressions against you that you need to forgive them of. This will allow you to get out all of your anger against everyone during one session.

c. As the Holy Spirit reminds you of their offenses, write down a list of all of them, even minor offenses. Don't try to hurry this step. Take your time and let the Holy Spirit speak to you. (When the Holy Spirit speaks to me I do not hear an "audible" voice, but insightful thoughts come to my mind which reveal things to me about myself and others that I was not previously aware of.)

6. Get your anger out.

　　a. Optional: Turn your list into a letter. Write a letter sharing everything each person has done to hurt you who you are trying to forgive. Write a letter and create a paragraph for each individual person, expressing everything they did which hurt you. Let it all out in the letter.

　　b. Or you may just use your list to prompt the conversation.

7. Place two chairs so they are facing each other, and sit in one of them. Imagine that the first person on your list or in your letter is now seated in the chair facing you. Share your

list or letter with that person. Again, don't stifle any emotions or strong language that accompanies the confessions. Say everything you are feeling.

8. Release each person. Make the choice by an act of your will to forgive each person once and for all. Say something like this: "Because I am forgiven and accepted by Christ, I can now forgive and accept you, _____, unconditionally in Christ. I choose now to forgive you, _____, no matter what you did to me. I release you from the the things you did which hurt me (name specifically what hurt you), and you are no longer accountable to me for them. You are now forgiven and I am now free."

9. Pray to God this prayer of faith: "Lord Jesus, as You have completely forgiven me of all of my sins, please help me to fully forgive and release _____ of all of their sins against me. By faith I receive Your unconditional love and acceptance in the place of this hurt, and I trust You to meet all my needs. Please help me take back the ground I have allowed Satan to gain in my life because of my attitude toward _____. Please give me peace, and help me to serve you. In Jesus' name I pray, Amen,"

10. DESTROY THE LETTER AND YOUR LISTS! This is an important step. It will not help you or others to come across these in the future.

11. Accept the person if they are still part of your life. Even if the feelings are not following just yet, take the action and realize the feelings will follow.

12. Realize God uses the sins of others to remind us of His grace to us. Thank Him for giving you a deeper appreciation of the depth of His love and forgiveness for us.

13. Pray for the person who hurt you. They did it because they have pain in their life. This does not mean that you should let them hurt you again. Protect yourself. But praying for them (and not a prayer that God will hurt them!) will help soften your heart.

This may sound a little eccentric to you, but it can be a very therapeutic activity. My counselor required me to do something similar. I wrote a letter and then I shared it with her. It did not automatically cure me, but it was huge step in moving me closer to forgiveness, and eventually I got to the point of complete forgiveness for this man and his family. You can read the details of my exercise in my journal entries in this chapter.

As difficult and uninviting as it is to deal with, we must realize that ultimately it is worse not to work through our anger and to fail to forgive those who have hurt us. It will result in bitterness, estranged relationships, isolation, and stress. We must force ourselves to deal with our feelings of anger and resentment when they occur. We must forgive others for our mental health and peace of mind. Although you may feel awkward participating in these two activities, they are crucial, therapeutic steps in the healing process.

> God created anger,
> and when used correctly,
> it does serve a purpose.

Journal Entries

November 10, 1991

Now when I think about the accident, I am so angry that the killer was drinking at a co-worker's child's birthday party. How could the host and others be so irresponsible as to let this guy drive when he was so drunk? They make me so mad. Not one of them even sent me a sympathy card. Cowards! What are they afraid of? Are they refusing to take responsibility, reasoning that if they admit their error, I might sue them? Is that how pathetic they are, that they do not even have the decency to say, "I'm sorry?"

I have so much anger toward the driver, too. The police report determined that he had been drinking all day long. He took the life of a good man: my husband, and my girls' father. I am furious that he was so careless, reckless, selfish and inconsiderate.

My counselor told me I need to vent my anger. As instructed, I wrote a letter to the killer. She said to say freely what I would want to say to him, even if it sounds hateful or includes cursing. She said to just be honest.

On my next visit I brought the letter to her office. What she did not tell me before was that she wanted me to read it aloud to her. I tried to just hand it to her, but she insisted, so finally, reluctantly, I read it. Through colorful language and strong emotion, I told him how much he has taken from me and how furious I am. The whole process was very emotional, and, once again, I am crying.

I even feel anger toward Gary for leaving me. I am mad that when

JOURNAL ENTRIES

he got to heaven he did not ask God to send him back down to us, because we need him here (as if he had any say). I am mad that he's lounging away in glory, while I am stuck down here, dealing with all of these hassles. I feel like when I see him in heaven, first I'm going to hug him, and then I'm going to punch him. I know that this is totally irrational, but right now I am not feeling overly rational.

One of the best, yet hardest "homework" assignments that I was given by my counselor was to work out my anger physically. I had to take a racquetball racquet and hit my mattress with it repeatedly for a minimum of twenty minutes, when I felt angry. Obviously I felt very awkward doing this, so I put it off. For the next few sessions, she kept asking me if I had done it, to which I replied, "Not yet." Finally she said, "Either do it this week at home or I will have you do it here in my office in front of me." That was all I needed. I felt way too self-conscious to do that, so I relented and beat on my mattress. I felt stupid, but I must admit I did feel better after doing it. I was able to do it in private, and not hurt anyone while releasing some of my anger.

January 3, 1992

THIS STINKS!! I hate this!! This is the worst time in my life and I need Gary now more than ever, but he can't be here. I feel so alone. I just came back from a party—let's just magnify the fact that I am no longer a couple. It was bad, I felt so different, so isolated from everyone else, on top of a crappy week I've had. I know my pain is showing. My annoyance shows. It's no fun to being around me. I just can't shake this crappy feeling.

It's hard to believe that three years ago this Sunday, I gave birth to Laurel. (Could her upcoming birthday be adding to my depression?) What a happy day that was. I remember it so vividly. I wish I was back at that time, with my little family and our humble surroundings. THIS STINKS!!

> **JOURNAL ENTRIES**

January 21, 1992

Tonight I started an intense weekly Bible study. What an excellent study! We are going through the Old Testament Minor Prophets. It's amazing how much we can relate to them. Tonight the speaker started her lecture by saying, "Maybe you are going through something unfair, maybe God has let something unfair happen to you," which I could relate to. She continued, giving the loss of a husband as an example of this, and later even mentioned an accident to demonstrate the brevity of life. Maybe God was trying to talk to me?!? The theme of her message was surrendering your heart to God and repenting from whatever He's trying to bring to your attention.

Lately, I've been experiencing a lot of anger. It seems to flare up quickly. I was at the grocery store the other day and the girls started acting up. It was nothing big, just childish behavior. But I could feel my anger escalating inside of me. Thankfully, just as I was exiting the store, I ran into an acquaintance who had lost her husband at a young age. It was as if God sent her to me. She just seemed to ask the right, poignant questions about how I was doing, and I gave her honest answers. She could relate, and at the end of our brief conversation, my anger had diffused. Usually I try to get my anger out when I can by hitting my bed with the racquet. Unfortunately, it does not always flare up

JOURNAL ENTRIES

at times when it is convenient to do this. I've noticed that even little things can really set me off.

Also, now, for the first time, I have some anxiety while driving. Why now, all of a sudden? I still do not remember the accident. I was a mess tonight as a passenger in a relative's car. I felt like every car was coming at us.

February 18, 1992

My anger must be so apparent! I get so mad at little things people do, but don't communicate it to them (which is probably saving my life). Like, tonight while I was driving in a parking lot, a guy cut me off. I wanted so badly to yell at him. The thing that motivated me to keep my mouth shut was, ironically, the fact that he saw where I parked, and I was afraid he might've keyed my car. (Whatever it takes, I guess, to keep from self-destructing). It took me a long time to cool down from that little incident.

February 22, 1992

The accident took place eight months ago, and there are many similarities between that day and today. Both days I worked hard all day, was thankful that the girls took long naps, took a shower about 5pm, ate pizza for dinner, and was supposed to go to Bible study, but didn't make it. Now it's 9:05 p.m.—Gary was still alive this time eight months ago. That fateful, crappy day: the worst day of my life. I wish he didn't have to die. I miss him so much.

Tonight I was supposed to go to Bible study, but I just didn't feel like going. Sometimes I'm just sick and tired of trying to make an effort and act like everything is okay, because it is not. I do not feel as low and hopeless as I did, but I'm still hurting. It hurts to see other couples so comfortable with each other. I wish it was me. I had what I wanted—a great family and a wonderful husband. It's like a bomb has exploded in the middle of my dream. I can't see the point of his death. I'm not better off and my girls are definitely NOT BETTER OFF!!

This is the worst thing that could happen to me—to lose a member of my little family. I always thought that no matter what happened, Gary and I could handle it together. Now here I am experiencing the @!*%est thing in my life, and I have to do it without him.

Of course, when I think like this, I need to count my blessings. First, that God didn't take my girls, too. I'd be suicidal if He had. Also, I'm SO thankful that Gary is in heaven, and I'll see him again. And I'm thankful I can stay home with my girls, and for my family, friends, and church.

March 26, 1992

I still have anger, which I have been avoiding working through, because it is so unpleasant. I wish God would just take my anger away from me, instantly. Just zap it out of me. I know He can do that. I'm guessing He would prefer for me to deal with it, and experience all of the lessons I will learn from it. Yay.

April 3, 1992

I have not written lately because I have not felt like it. However, I am paying for it; I have a loss of concentration and memory. Journaling

JOURNAL ENTRIES

helps those.

Other than that, I'd say I am doing better. We were housebound with the chicken pox for three weeks, since the girls had them one right after the other, and I was afraid I would go into depression, but I did not.

Also, I am coming out of my "fog" a little, and appreciating some of the ways my daughters are growing. They are very cute and keep me going.

My counselor said the reason I'm actually able to anticipate things is because I have been venting my anger (in a productive way) and that releases my other emotions, since suppressing one emotion results in suppressing them all.

April 26, 1992

Sometimes I think I am recovering from this and that I will make it and then I plunge low again. My feelings oscillate so much! Ironically, during the chicken pox quarantine, I felt the best since the accident, probably due to lots of prayer. But it has been shaky ever since then.

Tonight, there was a congregational meeting at church, and when I left I was so riled up. I guess it was a combination of things. There were many couples there without their children, sitting arm in arm. And I remembered how Gary and I used to come to meetings like this, and then go out to get a bite to eat afterward, a little "date." And there I sat with my two pre-schoolers, who were fairly good, but still antsy, and it took work to control them.

Well, I've been angry tonight at God and everything else. My house is a wreck because I really do not feel like straightening it up. It

Stage Seven: Anger and Resentment | 147

> **JOURNAL ENTRIES**

STINKS, STINKS, STINKS that I'm stuck here alone without Gary. I know he's not coming back. I can't believe that after knowing Gary for the last ten years of my life, I'm suddenly on my own again. How much longer am I going to be alone? Two years, ten years? I can't stand the thought of it. These are supposed to be some of the best years of my life, and I've been RIPPED OFF!

May 7, 1992

Laurel asks me often if Daddy can come down from heaven and come back to our house. It breaks my heart. How can she understand that he can't? It STINKS.

I am still dealing with a lot of anger now. I feel like a mess—my counselor is pleased. She says I am making progress, because it is coming out. Sometimes my adrenalin kicks way up and I get this nervous anxiety. Also, I find myself grinding my teeth. And my mind is constantly racing—jumping back and forth between so many different things. I'm having a hard time concentrating.

May 8, 1992

Both Mother's Day and my birthday are coming up. I've been ignoring the holiday, but it's coming anyway. Another day to accentuate the fact that Gary is not here. My sister was extremely thoughtful, though, and came to my house and had my girls give me a Mother's Day card and a gift. That was so kind of her. I cried.

I feel this rebellion in me toward my schedule. Lately I have been either arriving late to my appointments or just canceling them. I'm

JOURNAL ENTRIES

not motivated to do anything, especially when it involves making arrangements with other people. Like, tonight I was supposed to go to a concert at church, and I really felt like I should go, but I had no one to go with. So I stayed home, and I felt like crying, so I did. If things get complicated, I'd rather just bail out.

June 1, 1992

I'm still dealing with my anger but it is getting better, a little.

It seems that God is really molding and shaping me. He has revealed so many of my sins to me lately—sins I did not even know that I was guilty of. For instance, He has shown me my sin of pride, and how much of my self-worth is wrapped up in what I have, instead of who I am.

I was watching a movie the other day and at one point I laughed, and I was surprised at how foreign that felt to my face. I realized I must not have laughed, or even smiled, in a few days. I must not be a lot of fun to be around.

> One of the best, yet hardest "homework" assignments that I was given by my couselor was to work out my anger physically.

Practical Advice for the Anger and Resentment Stage

FOR THOSE WHO ARE GRIEVING:

1. Write it down. Often, a thought goes through our heads over and over again. The best way to release it is to write it down. Write a letter to the person with whom you are angry. Take my counselor's advice and feel free to be honest. Use vulgarity or colorful language if it helps you. One important step: When you are done writing down these emotions, *destroy the letter!*

PRACTICAL ADVICE

2. Release your anger. Admit that you have anger, and find a positive way to physically vent it, whether it is by hitting a mattress with a racquet, attacking a punching bag with boxing gloves, or performing some other harmless activity. Try Tae Bo, or take your anger out while practicing your tennis serve. I have a friend who gets out her anger while she's scrubbing her tub or oven. Find a way that works for you, but be sure to vent in a way that does not hurt others or yourself.

3. Be careful how you vent! Some ways you should not vent your anger are through your driving (don't we see enough of that already?), through your tennis, golf game, or any sport that you are playing with others that requires precision (it really messes up your score), or through similar activities. Basketball and other contact sports, such as football, may be helpful as long as you do not harm the other players or yourself.

4. Apologize when you overreact. When you overreact, and you will, humble yourself and tell those whom you have offended that you are sorry.

5. Work toward forgiveness. For your own peace of mind and sanity, I recommend you work through your anger so you can get to the place where you are able to forgive those who have hurt you. You may want to try the exercise given in this chapter to do this. Be honest with yourself during the process. If you are angry at God, admit it. He already knows it. Trust that He can help you work through it.

Practical Advice for the Anger and Resentment Stage

FOR FAMILY AND FRIENDS OF THOSE GRIEVING:

1. Encourage them to vent. In order to get through this stage they must deal with their anger. Getting their anger out by venting physically and writing letters can be very therapeutic. Encourage them to do it in a manner that does not harm others.

2. Persevere through the negativity. If they have become negative, try to stick with them. I know it is hard, but at the appropriate time, gently point out your observations of their behavior.

3. Forgive them. If they get angry with you, try to see past the anger, realizing the true cause. If their anger is unwarranted, try not to let it ruin your relationship.

> We need to find a way
> to physically release our anger
> without harming ourselves
> or someone else.

Bible Verses

TO COMFORT DURING THE ANGER AND RESENTMENT STAGE:

*My dear brothers, take note of this:
Everyone should be quick to listen,
slow to speak and slow to become angry,
for man's anger does not bring about
the righteous life that God desires.*
James 1:19-20

*Do not repay anyone evil for evil.
Be careful to do what is right in the eyes of everybody.
If it is possible, as far as it depends on you,
live at peace with everyone.
Do not take revenge, my friends,
but leave room for God's wrath, for it is written:
"It is mine to avenge; I will repay," says the Lord.
On the contrary: "If your enemy is hungry, feed him;
if he is thirsty, give him something to drink.
In doing this, you will heap burning coals on his head."
Do not be overcome by evil, but overcome evil with good.*
Romans 12:17-21

*A gentle answer turns away wrath,
but a harsh word stirs up anger.*
Proverbs 15:1

*A fool gives
full vent to his anger,
but a wise man
keeps himself under control.*
Proverbs 29:11

"In your anger do not sin:"
Do not let the sun go down while you are still angry,
and do not give the devil a foothold.
Ephesians 4:26-27

Whoever of you loves life
and desires to see many good days,
keep your tongue from evil
and your lips from speaking lies.
Psalm 34:12-13

The wise woman builds her house,
but with her own hands the foolish one tears hers down.
Proverbs 14:1

A hot-tempered person stirs up conflict,
but the one who is patient calms a quarrel.
Proverbs 15:18

An angry person stirs up conflict,
and a hot-tempered person commits many sins.
Proverbs 29:22

Love is patient, love is kind.
It does not envy, it does not boast, it is not proud.
It does not dishonor others, it is not self-seeking,
it is not easily angered, it keeps no record of wrongs.
Love does not delight in evil but rejoices with the truth.
1 Corinthians 13:4-6

OTHER
RECOMMENDED
BIBLE VERSES:
Amos 5:14-15a,
Proverbs 30:32-33

BIBLE VERSES

> Because of our loss,
> it is too painful to go back,
> and the changes we
> have undergone
> make our future seem
> scary and uncertain.

CHAPTER 10

STAGE EIGHT: GRADUAL ACCEPTANCE

As amazing as it may seem, if we are honest with ourselves, we find that we are often hesitant to return to our "normal" lives. We have become comfortable in our grief, and we resist returning to our previous way of living. Letting go of our grief makes us feel like we are minimizing our loss, and we definitely do not want to do that. Westberg (2012) explains,

> The reason our loss impacted us so tremendously was because we lost something special to us. We may feel that others have forgotten our tragedy, but we want to keep the memory alive. We do not want life to go back to "normal" (p. 64).

We fear going back to our former way of life. Because of our loss, it is too painful to go back, and the changes we have undergone make our future seem scary and uncertain. As much as we may despise this whole process, however, it is easier to stay here than to move on.

It is important for us to recognize this tendency, and make a conscious choice to move forward. Although we may dread some of the changes now in our lives, our future is not all bleak. God promises us, His children, that He has a plan for our lives. Jeremiah 29:11-13 reminds us of this: "For I know the plans I have for you," declares the Lord, "plans to prosper you and not to harm you, plans to give you hope and a future. Then you will call upon me and come and pray to me, and I will listen to you. You will seek me and find me when you seek me with all your heart." Many people focus on only verse 11 in this passage, but we need to include verses 12 and 13 as well, which tell of our responsibility here. The key is for us to seek God. God has not forgotten us, He still loves us (He never stopped), and He has a plan for us.

As we recognize this tendency and resolve we will move forward, we gradually begin to feel better. We are still expressing emotion, but it is neither as often nor as intense as it has been. We may be able to speak about our loss without becoming as emotional as we have in the past. We still may have days when we feel low and depressed, but they, too, are lessening. We begin to see a light at the end of the tunnel, although it may be dim at times.

How long it takes for us to get to this stage depends on our situation and our personality. Depending on the nature of our loss and our psychological makeup, it may take only a short time, or it may take over a year. The important thing is to work through our grief so we do get to this point.

We will not be the same as we used to be, because we will come out of this process as changed people. Hopefully, if we have worked through our grief and stayed close to God, we are changed for the better. Ideally, we have learned more about ourselves and deepened our faith and trust in God. He uses everything in our lives for His purposes, and He can use us and our loss for good. Westberg (2012) asserts,

> We finally begin to affirm reality. Please note that we do not say the final stage is, "We become our old selves again." When we go through any significant grief experience, we come out of it as different people. Depending upon the

> way we respond to this event, we are either stronger people than we were before or weaker; either healthier in spirit, or sicker (p. 71).

It is normal to feel far from victorious at this point. It has been a difficult road, and even if we do not feel like we have reacted to every situation in the way we would have liked, we need to be encouraged that God still loves us, and He still has work for us to do. We can always go to Him in prayer, confess the areas that we feel we failed in, and experience His sweet forgiveness.

When God finally spoke to Job (in Job 38-41), He never explained why He allowed Job to suffer. Instead, His divine discourses allowed Job to see God's goodness. We will probably not get an answer to why we had to experience our loss. While I am here on earth, I'll never understand why God took Gary. I know it is better for Gary, since he is now in heaven. I also know that if we truly love someone, then we want what is best for him, even if it hurts us. Instead of asking God, "Why?" perhaps we should ask, "What do You want me to learn from this?" It's highly likely we will get a thorough answer to that question.

Journal Entries

August 6, 1992

Just when I thought things were improving...My counselor is making me "release Gary." She had me write a letter to him telling him I am accepting him leaving me. I procrastinated (of course), finally doing it the night before my next counseling session. It was awful. Such a final step. I cried all night, and then was a mess the next day, too.

She said that I have a choice. I have progressed far in my grieving, and I can either stay here (not happy, more resentful than content) or I can move on, a painful but necessary process.

Part of this process includes selling my house, not wearing my wedding band anymore, getting rid of more reminders of Gary in my house (things that were his that I do not have a need for), and removing the rest of his clothes that I did not pack away. I'd gotten "comfortable" or at least somewhat accepted my role as his widow, but now she wants me to move to the point of realizing that I am a single parent.

It hurts so much because it is so final. She said it is normal to not want to do this, but I can't let my fears prevent me from moving forward.

August 30, 1992

I am finally feeling better—more "normal." I was crying about Gary the other night, but it was the first time in a long time, and it's hard to explain, but it wasn't as intense as before. And I am starting to feel happy for Gary instead of rejected and resentful for him "leaving me" (which is irrational, I know, since he did not have a choice, and God is in control, but I can't help it).

My counselor said I am ready to cut back my counseling to every other week.

Laurel and Lindsay are doing very well. Lindsay has been much happier lately, and not nearly as serious as she was. She talks all the time now, and her comprehension has really increased. Laurel acts so mature—sometimes it is like talking to another adult! She thinks she is, especially when it comes to dealing with her sister. Poor Lindsay—she doesn't have a father, but she has two mothers (Laurel and me)!

I am thankful that I have healed 100% from my physical wounds. I am spleen-less, but I have not felt any side effects from that. I am thankful to God that I am still able to be a stay-at-home mom for my daughters, and that I am physically able to take care of them.

One thing that had been "painfully therapeutic" was working with my mother-in-law to lead a grief support group through our church. We saw the need, contacted one of our pastors, and formed "The Comforting Shepherds." We met one night a month in one of our homes and invited anyone who was grieving (they did not have to be a church member to attend). Traditionally, the first time we had new visitors, they would spend some time sharing the details of their loss. Then we would each divulge what issues we had been dealing with for the past month. It was extremely difficult, and many tears were shed. We found that we almost dreaded going because it was so difficult (and many members would skip meetings if they were not up to it), but afterward we felt much better. After doing this for several months, we found that the need seemed to dwindle. It was helpful to us, and hopefully others, but when it was over, we were okay with that.

JOURNAL ENTRIES

Epilogue

Although that is the last journal entry included in this book, I didn't exactly ride off into the sunset, fully healed, after writing it. However, I did feel better gradually, which I was grateful for. I still went through a few valleys, but they weren't as deep or as frequent, and I didn't stay in them as long. During one of these, I begged my counselor to allow me to begin taking an anti-depressant, but she said I was so far along in my grieving that I did not need it. My grieving period lasted about eighteen months.

> We will not be
> the same as we used to be,
> because we will
> come out of this process
> as changed people.

Practical Advice for the Gradual Acceptance Stage

FOR THOSE WHO ARE GRIEVING:

1. Release your loved one. If your loss involved a death, when you get to this point, it's time to write a letter to let your loss go. This doesn't mean that you don't still love him, or that you are forgetting her. This means you are making a conscious decision to move forward in your life. Wouldn't our loved ones want us to do that? Don't you think they want us to be happy again? Don't you want to be happy again? Then I encourage you to write the letter.

2. Make plans. Now it is time to start making plans for your future. It is very important that you have some things to look forward to, especially if your loss has created a void in your life. Fill the void. Have you been thinking about taking a class, starting a new hobby or sport, or joining a club? We should not stay in our self-pity. There was a time when that was allowed in grieving, but now we must move on.

3. Comfort others. God allows us to go through our trials for many reasons. One is to help others who are in similar situations (2 Corinthians 1:3-5). You may meet other people who are experiencing similar losses. If God places someone like that in your life, ask Him how you can help them, and then do it.

4. Serve others. One of the best ways to get beyond ourselves is to serve others. There are many people in the world who are far worse off than we are. By reaching out to help them, not only do we provide assistance to others in need, but we get a sense of accomplishment and fulfillment when we use our time and talents for someone else.

5. Focus on neglected areas. If you gained weight during the grieving process, put off quitting a bad habit (like smoking), or have been tolerating any other comparatively minor issues in your life, this might be the time for you to deal with these. Dropping those extra pounds or bad habits may improve your health and increase your self-confidence. Consider taking care of these now.

PRACTICAL ADVICE

6. Remove some of their items. Moving forward means not living in the past. If you have several of your loved one's items still around, it's time to put them away. This doesn't mean that you have to get rid of them or put every item out of sight. However, you need to pack up the excess and store it. You can leave a few things out, but the majority needs to go. If you are a widow, you should consider taking your wedding band off. If you were contemplating a move, you may want to begin to start taking it seriously. These things not only help you, but they are also signs to others that you are healing and moving forward.

Practical Advice for the Gradual Acceptance Stage

FOR FAMILY AND FRIENDS OF THOSE GRIEVING:

1. Encourage them to move on. Encourage them to try new things and to make new friends. If they are reluctant, ask them, "Do you think that your loved one would want you to remain in your pain? Don't you think that he or she would want you to move on?" You might even offer to do something new with them, such as take some classes to learn a new skill or sport, or join a club (such as a health club, an organization, a singles group, or whatever is appropriate for them). Help them find some positive activities to engage in. Also, if they mention that they are considering breaking any bad habits that they let run rampant during their grieving period, encourage them to work on these now.

2. Keep the memory alive. It is a delicate balance to keep the memory of a loved one alive and yet encourage those who are grieving to move ahead. One way to do this is to refer to their loved one in conversations.

> Now is the time to start making plans for your future.

Bible Verses

TO COMFORT DURING THE GRADUAL ACCEPTANCE STAGE:

*Teach us to number our days,
that we may gain a heart of wisdom.
Relent, LORD! How long will it be?
Have compassion on your servants.
Satisfy us in the morning with your unfailing love,
that we may sing for joy and be glad all our days.
Make us glad for as many days as You have afflicted us,
for as many years as we have seen trouble.
May your deeds be shown to your servants,
your splendor to their children.
May the favor of the
Lord our God rest on us;
establish the work of our hands for us—
yes, establish the work of our hands.*
Psalm 90:12-17

*Praise be to the God and Father
of our Lord Jesus Christ,
the Father of compassion
and the God of all comfort,
who comforts us
in all our troubles,
so that we
can comfort those
in any trouble
with the comfort
we ourselves
have received from God.*
2 Corinthians 1:3-4

*There is a time for everything,
and a season for every activity under heaven:
a time to be born and a time to die,
a time to plant and a time to uproot,
a time to kill and a time to heal,
a time to tear down and a time to build,
a time to weep and a time to laugh,
a time to mourn and a time to dance,
a time to scatter stones and a time to gather them,
a time to embrace and a time to refrain,
a time to search and a time to give up,
a time to keep and a time to throw away,
a time to tear and a time to mend.
a time to be silent and a time to speak,
a time to love and a time to hate,
a time for war and a time for peace.*
Ecclesiastes 3:1-8

*I waited patiently for the LORD; He turned to me and heard my cry.
He lifted me out of the slimy pit, out of the mud and mire;
he set my feet on a rock and gave me a firm place to stand.
He put a new song in my mouth, a hymn of praise to our God.
Many will see and fear And put their trust in the LORD.
Blessed is the man who makes the LORD his trust,
who does not look to the proud, to those who turn aside to false gods.
Many, O LORD my God, are the wonders you have done.
The things you planned for us
no one can recount to you; were I to speak and tell of them,
they would be too many to declare.*
Psalm 40 1-5

OTHER RECOMMENDED BIBLE VERSES:
Psalm 16, Psalm 34

BIBLE VERSES

> ...I am deeply grateful to God and my family, friends and long-suffering couselor for their patience, love and support during my grieving period.

FINAL WORDS

I hope this book has helped and encouraged you, whether you have experienced a loss or you desire to help someone you love who is grieving.

Although the process was arduous and long, I am happy to report that God helped me work through my grief and I am able to experience joy and contentment again. I am not perfect and still experience some of the emotions in the grieving process from time to time due to the loss of my husband. However, I am deeply grateful to God and my family, friends and long-suffering counselor for their patience, love and support during my grieving period. God enabled me to forgive the man who killed my husband, and I hope his family has been able to recover from their grief, as well, and move on with their lives. God has also blessed me with two wonderful daughters and allowed me to achieve many amazing goals that I never dreamed I would accomplish. I look forward to seeing Gary in heaven (I no longer plan to punch him when I see him!), and I also look forward to doing God's work here on Earth until I get there.

God created a new life for me, and He will do the same thing for you, too, if you let Him. My hope for you is that during this process you have seen God work in your life. I also hope you have gained a deeper understanding of yourself during this process. Please allow Him to triumph in and through you during this challenging time. You will probably not be the same person, but in many ways you will be stronger and wiser. May God bless you.

Warm Regards,

Tammy Hoffman

REFERENCES

Anderson, H. (2009, Aug 25). Common grief, complex grieving. *Pastoral Psychology* (59) 2.127-136.

Byron, T. (2007, Jul 02). My grieving daughter. *The Times*. Retrieved from http://search.proquest.com/docview/319780693?accountid=10902.

Geisler, N.L. (1996). How can we know the Bible is the word of God? In D.C. Halverson (Ed.), *The compact guide to world religions* (pp. 252-266). Minneapolis, MN: Bethany House Publishers.

Grieving comes in stages. (2009, April 3). *Gulf News*. Retrieved from http://go.galegroup.com.

Harrison, P. (1992). Grieving: Keep the process moving. *Canadian Family Physician,* 38, 683-683.

Huntington's Disease Society of America. (2014). Retrieved from http:// www.hdsa.org/images/content/1/3/13080.pdf

McDowell, J. (2011). Old Testament: Significance of Dead Sea scrolls. Retrieved from https://www.josh.org.

Phillips, R. & Talty, S. (2013). *A Captain's Duty: Somali pirates, Navy SEALS, and dangerous days at sea.* Hyperion e book.

Scott, N. (1992, Nov 22). The End of a Business Can Trigger the Normal Stages of Grieving Over a Loss: Final Edition. *The Sun*. ISSN 1930-8965

Stages in grieving process. (2007, Jun 13). *The Press and Journal*. Retrieved from http://ezproxy.fau.edu/login?url=http://search.proquest.com/docview/334084503?accountid=10902.

Stanley, C. (2002). 13 steps to forgiving the unforgiveable, from, *The gift of forgiveness.* Retrieved from http://www.cbn.com/spirituallife/prayerandcounseling/stanley_forgiveness.aspx

Suicide Awareness Voices of Education. (2014). Retrieved from http://www.save.org.

Westberg, G.E. (2012). *Good grief.* Minneapolis: Fortress Press.

Wood, T. (1995). Sometimes He calms the storm (recorded by Scott Krippayne). On *Wild imagination* (CD). Nashville, TN: Word Entertainment LLC.